A BLOODY
DAY

A BLOODY DAY

THE IRISH AT WATERLOO

DAN HARVEY

MERRION
PRESS

First published in 2017 by
Merrion Press
10 George's Street
Newbridge
Co. Kildare
Ireland
www.merrionpress.ie

© 2017, Dan Harvey

9781785371264 (paper)
9781785371271 (PDF)
9781785371424 (Kindle)
9781785371431 (epub)

British Library Cataloguing in Publication Data
An entry can be found on request

Library of Congress Cataloging in Publication Data
An entry can be found on request

Cover design by www.phoenix-graphicdesign.com

Cover front: Henri Félix Emmanuel Philippoteaux, *The Battle of Waterloo:
The British Squares Receiving the Charge of the French Cuirassiers*, 1874
(GL Archive/Alamy Stock Photo)

Printed in Ireland by SPRINT-print Ltd

DEDICATION

The Irish engagement with the Battle of Waterloo was of some considerable significance. They were good soldiers, fought well, and in no small measure helped Wellington earn his victory. This book is dedicated to those 'forgotten Irish' who fought, bled, and died at the Battle of Waterloo.

AUTHOR'S NOTE

I am a military man, so I have a mission in choosing to write this account of the Battle of Waterloo. It is primarily to raise an awareness that there were native-born soldiers from Ireland on the battlefield; next, to offer a deeper understanding of why this participation was so large and prominent; and finally, Waterloo examined through an 'Irish' lens sees it exemplifying how Ireland's heritage has been constructed historically. Ireland's heritage is about its identity, and the Battle of Waterloo was an exciting episodic event which enlivens an examination of this identity, placed, as it is, in the context of the creation of a modern Europe.

PREFACE

There is one past, but many histories. There was one Battle of Waterloo, but many versions. There was one Anglo-Allied Army, but many nationalities. There was one outcome, but many unknowns. One of the biggest unknowns was that many Irishmen participated. The Battle of Waterloo is itself a good story, highly dramatic, hard-fought, the outcome of which was in the balance to its very end. The story of the part played by the Irish is equally enthralling and must necessarily mention an 'Irish' presence, an 'Irish' prominence and an 'Irish' pride of participation. There was one Wellington, and many other Irish.

At mid-afternoon on the 18 June 1815 in the valley below the ridge of Mont-St-Jean near the Belgian village of Waterloo, Irishman Major General Sir William Ponsonby K.C.B of Imokilly, County Cork, commander of the 2nd British Cavalry (Union) Brigade was killed during a cavalry change. Later in the day, and on the ridge of Mont-St-Jean, Major Arthur Rowley Heyland from Castle Roe, Count Derry, was killed in action at the close of battle while leading the 1st Battalion of the 40th (2nd Somersetshire) Regiment of Foot. Arthur Rowley was buried near to where he fell on the battlefield of Waterloo. One of those who continued to contribute to lead the 40th Foot's steadfast defence of an exposed position was Captain Conyngham Ellis from Abbeyfeale, County Limerick. Two years later, Conyngham Ellis, now a major, died of wounds received at Waterloo.

Determined not to be forgotten in the event of his death during the up-coming campaign, later called the 'Hundred Days' campaign because of the time between Napoleon's escape from Elba and his final exile to St Helena, Ensign (Second-Lieutenant) Edward Hodder from Fountainstown, near Crosshaven, County Cork, carved his name on about a dozen beech trees along the back avenue to the farm on which he was raised. (He carved the words 'E. Hodder Fountainstown 1815'. The trees have nearly all gone now, but there are still a couple of them standing and when pointed out, the carving is still possible to see.) Edward Hodder survived the battle but was wounded and lost a leg. The story, still within the family today, is that when he returned without his leg he built himself a wheelchair and wheeled himself down to the beach in Fountainstown regularly, a distance of a mile. On his way back he would bring stones from the beach and he eventually built himself a path that enabled him to wheel himself to the farm's walled garden. He died in 1868.

Edward Costello, born in Mountmellick, County Laois, in 1788 enlisted with the 95th Rifles as a private soldier in 1807 and subsequently saw extensive service in the Peninsular War (1808-1814) and at Waterloo. He wrote a memoir of his service, *The Adventures of a Soldier* (London 1852). His memoir is a valuable record of this period, not only as one of comparatively few Irish military accounts, but due to its coming from an enlisted man, rare in a period when the average British army private soldier was illiterate. Officers' memoirs and journals tended to dominate instead.

On 23 April 1845, as an in-patient of the Royal Hospital Kilmainham, Dublin, James Graham from County Monaghan died. On the occasion, a number of British newspapers and journals published fulsome obituaries of the ex-soldier, formerly of the Light Company, 2nd Battalion, Coldstream Guards, describing him as 'the bravest of the brave at Waterloo', a tribute paid to very few common soldiers of the era.

In March 1892 in the town of Sherbrooke in the province of Quebec, Canada, 97-year-old Irishman Maurice Shea from County Kerry died. Born at Prior near Tralee in 1795, he enlisted in the British army and fought at the Battle of Waterloo as a private in Number Nine Company of the Second Battalion of the 73rd Highlanders. Maurice Shea continued to serve with the 73rd until leaving the army as a corporal in 1822. He eventually settled in Canada, living there until his death. He was generally credited as being the last surviving British veteran of the Battle of Waterloo.

Arthur Wesley, later Field Marshal Arthur Wellesley, 1st Duke of Wellington, a ninth generation member of the Colley Family who settled in Ireland about 1500 (while the first of the Wellesleys is believed to have arrived earlier around 1170 with Henry II) was a native of Dangan Castle near Trim, County Meath. Born in Dublin, he was baptised Arthur Mornington in St Peter's Church, Dublin, on 30 April 1769. Commissioned in 1787, he commanded British forces in India and the Iberian Peninsula and was appointed officer-in-charge of the Anglo-Allied (British, Dutch, German, Belgian) army at the Battle of Waterloo.

One third of the Anglo-Allied army at Waterloo were British, and one third of these were, like Wellington himself, Irish. Yet such a substantial Irish participation in a dramatic event that decided the fate of Europe, a turning point in history, is neither immediately nor readily brought to mind by the British nor indeed by the Irish themselves when mention is made of the battle.

Irishmen in their thousands from every county, walk of life, and corner of society in Ireland were present and active on the battlefield of Waterloo. Whether participating in specifically designated Irish units or as sizeable proportions of many, if not most, British units with absolutely no formal Irish affiliation, they were involved in all the battle's significant actions. Like himself, a number of Wellington's key subordinates in his command and control structure as brigade commanders were Irish. This was true also of the next hierarchical level in Wellington's chain-of-command, with Irishmen among his battalion and regimental commanders. Irish officers liberally populated these battalion and regimental establishments, and others held important central staff and support appointments.

These Irish were there when the irresistible force of Napoleon's Armée de Nord (Army of the North) hit Wellington's immovable defensive line along the ridge of Mont-St-Jean on the compressed battlefield of Waterloo, with hostilities commencing at 35 minutes past eleven on 18 June 1815. At stake was the future shape of Europe. Repeated, determined attacks throughout the day met a stiff stubborn defence, resulting in carnage. Wellington had nailed himself to the ridge and Napoleon threw everything he had to move him off it. Deadly assaults against a desperate defence. Concentrated artillery bombardments, close-quarter volleys of infantry musket-fire, courageous cavalry charges, all tore blood from flesh, flesh from bone, bone from body, and breath from life. There was bloodshed, mutilation, and violent death on both sides. Napoleon unleashed multiple cannonades, massive columns of infantry, and massed cavalry to smash Wellington's will by sheer weight of numbers, while the latter replied with staunch defence and ferocious counter-attacks. Both generals knew the battle would be decisive. Both were highly skilled, experienced commanders in the field. Neither had faced the other before. Both were winners, but one must lose. The space over which the battle raged was compact, the battle space densely populated, and time was critical. The battlefield was 5 kilometres long and 3 kilometres wide. There were 180,000 troops, 35,000 horses and 500 cannons on it. It was a fiercely fought and formidable battle. Both commanders were determined to win, and each possessed the wit and lethal means to achieve it. The result was an enormous cost in dead and wounded. Many Irish were amongst the battle's casualties. Of the Irish wounded at Waterloo, there were many who recovered with little ill effects; others were maimed for life; and others still did not rally from wounds received, dying days, weeks, months, even years later. Of those among the fatalities, most were buried at Waterloo. The overall extent of the casualties on all sides was staggering, the Irish suffering severely. When the battle's death toll was increasing by the minute, its outcome far from decided, at day's end with dusk descending, both armies shattered and near collapse, they remained evenly matched. With the issue still deadlocked, the battle in the balance, the fighting continuing, the Prussians arriving in force from the east, the French pressed harder and the bodies literally mounted. Standing with Wellington, holding the line with the battle-shocked, exhausted, and battered Anglo-Allies, only just, and at enormous cost were thousands of soldiers from Ireland, fighting bravely. This is their story.

CONTENTS

List of Illustrations

List of Maps

INTRODUCTION

IF THERE is a place on earth that has defined its identity against the British, it is Ireland. So how was it that the Irish whom the British suppressed for centuries should have contributed so much to the Waterloo campaign and why has this participation largely escaped notice to date?

Ireland's involvement in the Waterloo campaign was significant. The Irish engagement with this hugely historic epic event at the turn of the 19th century has yet to become popularly appreciated and properly applauded. Thousands of Irish soldiers both by birth and descent were eagerly engaged on the battlefield, among the ranks, high up, and all the way throughout the chain-of-command, some even conspicuous by individually noteworthy and otherwise gallant actions. Overall, the presence, posture, and performance of the Irish at the Battle of Waterloo is a proud and compelling story.

The Irish involvement at the Battle of Waterloo is a true story which has not figured prominently, if at all, in the cultural narrative of an independent Ireland to-date. It has been a story lost within the accounts of the magnificence of the suspense, the anxious uncertainty, the excitement of the action, central to the relating of the causes, course, and consequences of the battle itself. It is timely and important at the book's outset to remind ourselves of the magnitude of such an encounter. The battle was a hostile confrontation involving vast groups using lethal means. It was the violent imposition of will, one man's madness manifest in might proving right. The battle was raw, frightening and ugly, it was noisy, bloody and confused. It was the ruthless killing in great numbers of its participants. It was where the feared momentum of a French attacking manoeuvre met the steely strength of Anglo–Allied static defence, a thrusting energy hitting unyielding resilience, impetus against steadfastness. Butchery was done and slaughter resulted. The attrition of hideous death was horrible and widespread, the woundings atrocious. Heads, bodies, and arms were atomised by cannon balls, the brutal breaking of bone, mangling of limbs and torsos, men and horses, the extinguishing of precious lives by the arbitrary disintegration of bodily structures immense. In the midst of this maelstrom soldiers stood or advanced in columns and awaited their individual fate, with fate itself deciding. There was courage and cowardice; mercy and cruelty; impetuousness and procrastination; panic and calmness; clarity and confusion; organisation and disorganisation; there was good, bad, and no leadership, and there were momentary misunderstandings and miscommunications leading to momentous mistakes. Napoleon said he lost Waterloo because of the 'obstinate bravery of the British troops' (thousands being Irish). Wellington said of the 1st Battalion of the 27th Inniskillings, 'they saved the centre of my line'. Napoleon said of them, 'I have seen Russian, Prussian, and French bravery, but anything to equal the stubborn bravery of the regiment with castles in their caps, I have never witnessed.'

Wellington has often been quoted (and criticised) for describing his soldiers as 'the scum of the earth', but seldom quoted was his proud addition, 'it is really wonderful that we should have made them the fine fellows they are'. It was the raw material he was referring to, how the men presented on enlistment, not the finished article, the trained soldier, disciplined, drilled, with a noted proficiency for 'clockwork musketry' while standing steady, staunch, and silent. He was particularly proud of his Peninsular War participants, the backbone of whom were largely Irishmen. Wellington often said of this army that it was one with which 'I could have done anything'. This Peninsular War army, on the war's cessation in 1814, was largely dispersed to North America, Ireland, and the West Indies, however, and significantly, Wellington had available to him a sufficient portion of them come June 1815. In a Brussels park just before the opening of the Waterloo campaign proper, Wellington was asked by a companion (a British parliamentarian named Thomas Creevey) with whom he was walking about the possible outcome of the approaching hostilities. Wellington pointed to an off-duty British infantryman who happened to stroll by, and said, 'There, it all depends upon that article whether we do business or not. Give me enough of it (them), and I am sure.' In the event, he was just about to have 'enough of them' on the field of Waterloo, and just 'enough of them' were Irish.

Ireland, the Irish, and an exploding Europe

Saltpetre, sulphur, and charcoal combined is an explosive mix called gunpowder. This black blend of chemical substances resulted in a new and devastatingly effective technology that revolutionised European warfare, bringing about a complete rethinking of defence works and battlefield tactics. More especially, massed infantry with muskets closely packed in huge formations now dominated the battlefield. Massed musket volleys allied with artillery cannon shot could decide the outcome of battles.

Manufacturing gunpowder was a difficult, dangerous process and involved many skills. Ballincollig Royal Gunpowder Mills in County Cork was one of three Royal gunpowder mills that manufactured gunpowder to meet the demands of the British army during the Napoleonic Wars. In close proximity to Cork City and one of the world's largest natural harbours, second only to Sydney, the gunpowder mill was of great strategic importance. Originally opened in 1794 as a private enterprise producing blasting powder for construction works, mining, and quarrying, the mills attracted the attention of the British Board of Ordnance after the 1798 Rebellion, and on its purchase in 1805 was expanded tenfold with 12 new mills added to the complex, as well as new processing buildings and homes for the workers. Security was an issue, and a cavalry barracks was constructed in 1810, its garrison providing military escorts for the wagons of gunpowder to Cork harbour. With its multitude of ports and harbours and its access to shipping routes to Europe, North America, and elsewhere, Ireland had always been well situated to facilitate the strategic movement of British forces around the world. There was a reverse side to this. Philip II of Spain had once said, 'If England you wish to gain, with Ireland you must begin'. In 1601, Don Juan d'Aquilla was dispatched with a Spanish expedition to Ireland and together with the Irish was narrowly defeated at the Battle of Kinsale, County Cork. The lesson was not lost on the English and they held onto Ireland mainly for military reasons. Two centuries later, as the 19th century dawned, the British empire and France were engaged in a brutal war. The armies of France, forged in the turmoil of the French Revolution and under the brilliant leadership of Napoleon Bonaparte, had won repeated victories against the Ottoman Empire, Austria, Prussia, and Russia. With the continent under French control, the threat of invasion now hung over Britain. Only the English Channel protected the British from their age-old enemies. To counter this perceived threat, the government of King George III increased military garrisons and strengthened fortifications throughout Britain and Ireland.

Group of Cavalry in the Snow by Jean Louis Ernest Meissonier, 1815-1891,
National Gallery of Ireland.

The French in Killala Bay by William Sadler the Younger,
National Gallery of Ireland.

The Robust engaging The Hoche off Tory Island by John Thomas,
National Gallery of Ireland.

Special consideration was given to the defences of Ireland, as French strategy in recent years had been to incite and assist armed rebellion by means of military intervention. In 1796, Theobald Wolfe Tone, a leader in the United Irishmen organisation, attempted to land in Bantry Bay, County Cork, with a force of 15,000 men and 43 ships provided by France and commanded by the French General Lazare Hoche. The invasion fleet arrived in Bantry Bay on the evening of 21 December. Soon after its arrival, and before the troops could disembark, bad weather intervened in the shape of storm force winds that drove the ships out to sea again. In the climatic year of 1798 Ireland once again featured in the French war plans. On 22 August three ships containing a force of 1,100 men commanded by General Jean-Joseph Humbert landed in Killala Bay, County Mayo, their orders to make contact with the United Irishmen and assist them in establishing an independent Irish republic. Humbert and his Irish allies defeated a British force sent to stop them at the Battle of Castlebar. The subsequent retreat of the British forces became known to the locals as 'The Castlebar

Races'. Humbert's triumph was destined to be short-lived; a British force commanded by Lord Cornwallis met and defeated his army at the Battle of Ballinamuck on 8 September.

Watching events from France, Wolfe Tone was disappointed but not discouraged by the failed invasion. Once again he sought and received military assistance from the French. On 16 September 1798, a French fleet numbering nine ships holding 3,000 troops set sail from Brest. Again disaster struck. The French invasion force was intercepted by a British fleet commanded by Sir John Warren off the Donegal coast on 12 October. Bitter fighting ensued, lasting some ten hours, the result of which was an overwhelming British victory. Without the loss of a single ship, Sir John Warren captured seven ships and about 2,500 French troops. Among those captured was Theobald Wolfe Tone, who had travelled under the *nom de guerre* 'Adjutant General Smith'. In view of these events, the British government was determined to forestall any further invasion and occupation of Ireland. To this effect, garrisons were increased and fortifications strengthened throughout the county with an emphasis on strategic locations.

In 1803 Napoleon began assembling his invasion force in north-eastern France. Napoleon's Irish Legion, Legion Irlandaise, was formed in November of that year in Morlaix, Brittany. The Irish Legion (as it was to evolve, the forerunner of the French Foreign Legion) was created with a view to concurrent landings in Ireland and England, when a locally recruited force in Ireland would take up arms on its arrival. This would open up a second front, a simultaneous point of attack in a co-ordinated offensive on Britain Any unrest caused by Robert Emmet's Rising of 1803 was short-lived, largely confined to Dublin, and did not ignite the hoped-for insurrection. This was not to dampen the on-going planning and preparations of the Legion, and throughout early 1804 it continued to recruit, train, and prepare. However, in August 1805, the British naval victory by Admiral Nelson's fleet over that of the French at Trafalgar, where more than 30 per cent of Nelson's sailors were Irish, removed the possibility of invasion. Napoleon turned his army eastwards and marched them towards Austria. Victories over the Austrians and Russians at Austerlitz in December 1805 and the Prussians at Jena in 1806 saw him continue to hold sway on the continent. If Napoleon could not invade Britain he could blockade her; after all, it was an island and supplies could be prevented from arriving if they were stopped from being exported in the first place at their ports of origin. Napoleon attempted to extend his influence over England's trading partners and to effect a blockade that would cut off her supplies. However, while many countries approved of his values for self-determination, interfering with their trade was another matter and seen as taking a step too far. In any event, the Spanish requested assistance from Britain. Following the French invasion and occupation of Spain in May 1808, the Spanish authorities appealed to Britain for 'aid to rescue them from this flagrant usurpation of Bonaparte'. On receipt of this appeal it was decided that a force being assembled in Cork under Wellesley to assist the defence of the Spanish colonies in South America would go instead to Portugal, thus starting a campaign that became known as 'the Peninsular War'. Of the force that was placed under his command, the following units assembled in Cork and were quartered on the outskirts of the city: 1st Battalion 5th Foot, 1st Battalion 40th Foot, 1st Battalion 91st Foot, 1st Battalion 9th Foot, 5th Battalion 60th Foot, 4 Companies 95th Foot, 1st Battalion 38th Foot, 1st Battalion 71st Foot, and 4th Royal Veterans' Battalion.

On his arrival in Cork, Wellington lost little time in sending dispatches to Viscount Castlereagh, the Secretary of State; to

Lieutenant General Floyd, commanding at Cork; and to Lieutenant Cheeseman, RN, Resident Agent of Transport, Cork. These dispatches concerned the equipping and transportation of 444 officers, 552 sergeants, 227 drummers, 9,505 rank and file and 215 horses, which were to embark from 'Cove' under his command. The force embarked on 13 July 1808 and set sail for Portugal.

The Peninsular War (1807-1814) stands as one of the longest campaigns in British military history. Irish participation was pivotal. Ireland provided Wellington with a large proportion of his infantry, which played an important part in the persistent, painstaking pushing of the French from the Iberian Peninsula of Portugal and Spain, then up into southern France. Two Irish cavalry squadrons fought in the Peninsular War but their participation was far less than the infantry. Wellington's Irish Battalions consisted of three battalions of the 27th Foot (Inniskillings), and a battalion from each of the 83rd Foot, 87th Foot (Prince of Wales's Own Irish), 88th Foot (Connaught Rangers), and a brief appearance from the 89th Foot (The Princess Victoria's). In addition to these seven Irish infantry battalions continually present in the Peninsula, the non-Irish regiments had an average 35 per cent of Irishmen. The national composition of a battalion varied from year to year, according to casualties, recruitment, and transfers, so there was between 8 and 50 per cent Irish varying throughout the overall duration of the war. The 57th Foot (West Middlesex) had 34 per cent native Irish in 1809, many of whom had been recruited in the London area. The 29th Foot (Worcestershire) had 19 per cent in 1809. rising to 37 per cent in 1811. The 28th Foot (North Gloucestershire) had 40 per cent, a figure reputedly shared by the Royal Artillery. The 94th Foot (The Scots' Brigade) at one point contained the highest percentage of Irish, just over 51 per cent. 'Elite' light infantry battalions, the 43rd (Monmouthshire), the 52nd (Oxfordshire), and the 95th (Rifles), had about 25 per cent Irish. Most recruits came from the Catholic population.

'The Inniskillings' or the 27th Inniskillings were one of the strongest units in the British army during the Napoleonic period and one of the very few from 1812 on to have three battalions simultaneously in the Peninsula, mustering 4,078 men in 1810. The 3rd Battalion was the most heavily engaged, spending 64 complete months in that theatre. The 27th is also one of the oldest regiments, raised in 1689 during the Williamite Wars for the defence of the town of Enniskillen, and was originally known as Tiffin's Inniskilling Regiment, named after its first Colonel, Zachariah Tiffin. In 1751, the regiment became the 27th Foot and served in the Seven Years War (1756-63) in North America and the West Indies. It formed part of the British force in Alexandria (Egypt) in 1801, and in 1806 the First Battalion of the 27th fought at Maida, and with the second and third Battalions formed part of the Peninsula army, gaining battle honours at Badajoz, Salamanca, Vitoria, Pyrenees, Nivelle, Orkey, and Toulouse. The 3rd Battalion was the first of the three battalions to enter the Peninsular War in November 1808, the 1st Battalion entering in November 1812 and the 2nd Battalion a month later. The 1st Battalion, with a composition from 27 counties of origin throughout Ireland, went on to fight at Waterloo under the command of Major John Hare (6th Division, 10th Brigade). At half past six in the evening, the French, capturing the farmhouse strong-point of La Haye Sainte ('The Holy Hedge'), brought up field horse artillery and shredded the Anglo-Allied line at a range of less than 300 metres. Deployed in square at the junction of the Ohain and the Brussels-Charleroi crossroads, the 1st Battalion 27th Foot, 747 strong at daybreak, sustained 493 casualties or 66 per cent, reportedly the highest of any battalion.

The forces which Wellington led in Portugal and Spain and up into southern France between 1808 and 1814 achieved a consistent record of victory perhaps unmatched in the history of the British army. Put together, the Irish regiments and the Irish in non-Irish regiments made up some 40 per cent of this volunteer army, a remarkable figure given the bloodshed of the recent unrest of the 1798 Rebellion in Ireland and to a far lesser extent that of 1803. The size of the Irish contingent was out of proportion to Ireland's share of the United Kingdom's total population, especially as most Irish troops were drawn from Ireland's Catholic population. Officers of Irish birth or strong Irish connections, which may have been as great as one third of the officer corps, came mainly from Ireland's Anglican community of much less than one million, or about seven per cent of the population, but Catholic officers were appearing in increasing numbers.

Why did such recruits become available? Provoked by the American and French Revolutions, the Catholic Relief Acts of 1778 and 1782 abolished many restrictions on Catholics and began to bring them into the mainstream of British and Irish life. The 1793 Act in Ireland had amongst its supporters the Member of Parliament for Trim, County Meath, Arthur Wellesley, aged 24, later 1st Duke of Wellington. This act changed Ireland dramatically by enfranchising Catholics and giving them the heretofore denied access to the professions and to higher education. It also allowed Catholics once again to bear arms and to enter the armed forces legitimately, resulting in vast numbers swelling the rank and file, and so was a major factor in providing troops for the Revolutionary and Napoleonic Wars. It was not simple altruism or the need to reduce dissatisfaction in the wake of the French Revolution that motivated the Protestant Parliament in Dublin to restore the right to bear arms, but the pressing need to employ the well-established military talents of the Irish. As soon as the measure became law, regiment after regiment, hungry for recruits, sent parties to Ireland to recruit. It soon became impossible for a regiment to have served in Ireland not to have a strong Irish element. Recruiting parties found thousands of fit and tough young men only too eager to embrace the military life and escape the arduous living conditions and the problems caused by the lack of education, opportunity, and employment in an increasing population. Indeed, it was a policy to garrison a 'skeleton' battalion in Ireland after great losses from yellow fever in the West Indies to build up strength again. In 1797, for example, of the seven regular regiments of foot on the Irish establishment, five had recently returned from the West Indies, and were 'skeleton' units, busily recruiting.

The year 1795, two years after the outbreak of war with France, saw the formation of Ireland's most controversial force, the Irish Militia, at a strength of 18,000, which was increased to 28,000 in 1798. With its sister forces in England and Scotland, the Irish Militia was to have a major impact on the make-up and performance of the British armed forces between 1798 and 1815. With a majority of the infantry of the line (regular army) being Irish, could their loyalty be counted on? When it came to suppressing the 1798 Rebellion, only regiments with an overwhelming proportion of non-Irish troops were sent, such as the 100th Highlanders, later the 92nd Gordon Highlanders, and the 5th Battalion of the 60th (Royal American), composed mainly of Germans. The greater part in the suppression of the rebellion was played by the Irish Militia and by Fencible regiments from Scotland, such as the Stratspey Fencibles. From 1799, various Militia Transfer Acts enabled militiamen to transfer to their chosen line regiment up to a maximum of 15 per cent of the strength of the militia unit each year. Further acts enabled extra transfers in certain years. These transfers were commonplace, and Ireland often surpassed England and Scotland in numbers of volunteers or in percentage of quota achieved. Although recruitment by other methods continued, militia transfers were far more important, delivering to the army a supply of trained and ready troops. Overall, the extent of Irish recruitment in the British Army was impressive. Between 1793 and 1815, as many as 200,000 may have enlisted, many of whom found their way to the Peninsula with Wellington.

Napoleon's firm grip on the Continent of Europe and beyond began to slip as he over-reached, and after 15 years of continuous and glorious victories for France, his disastrous 10-month Russian campaign in 1812 was compounded by outright defeat against four European states at the three-day Battle of Leipzig in 1813. With Wellington's army pushing up from the south and those of Austria, Prussia, and Russia moving in from the east, Napoleon was forced to abdicate and was exiled on the Mediterranean Island of Elba. Europe was at peace. However, like the explosive mix of saltpetre, sulphur, and charcoal that was gunpowder, the destabilising ingredients of Napoleon's unquenched adventurous ambition was set to once again ignite, suddenly and sharply, and the Continent once more exploded into war.

PRELUDE TO BATTLE

The Congress of Vienna

THE RATTLE and rumpus of horseshoes together with the clanking and clatter of carriage wheels on the fashionable cobbled-stoned streets around the grand main entrance to Vienna's lavish Hofburg Palace were momentarily drowned out by the loud pealing of bells from St Michaels, the parish church of the courts. The ringing reverberated over the domed roofs of the four and five-storey buildings then repeated as an echo around the city walls and through the elegantly decorated shop-fronted streets, the courtyards, squares and parks. The magnificent grandeur of the palace, a vast complex that was the former Emperor of Austria's residence, was a permanent reminder of the glory of the Hofburg Empire. The royal apartments and buildings were in different styles, gothic, renaissance and baroque, and were an ornamental extravagance on a grand scale. Now it was an imperial forum playing host to the Congress of Vienna, a conference of delegates and dignitaries of European states who had come together in September 1814 to forge a new, and peacefully arrived at, balance of power in Europe. With Napoleon defeated and exiled in Elba, it was the perfect time to redraw the map of Europe. But only if they could agree to it. Six months on, in March 1815, the congress had in truth become deadlocked. Britain, Austria, and Bourbon France found themselves at variance with Prussia and Russia. Prussia wanted to annex Saxony, and Russia wanted Poland, the Tsar, Alexander I, himself overseeing Russian interests. Nearby, within hearing distance of the bells of St. Michael's, Arthur Wellesley, 1st Duke of Wellington, famous victor of the Peninsular War, had the month previous replaced Robert Stewart, Viscount Castlereagh, as senior British representative. Wellington had become frustrated by the stalemate and this morning, 7 March 1815, he was undertaking not more negotiations, but rather preparations for a hunting trip on the grounds of Schönbrunn Palace. Busily overseeing final preparations before departure, he was interrupted by the dramatic news that 'the Monster', 'the Werewolf', the 'Corsican Ogre', Napoleon, had escaped from Elba, landed in France, and that the army and the people were flocking to his support. Wellington would be hunting bigger prey than he had imagined. The 'Devil' was unchained and required re-capturing!

'An Enemy of Humanity'

Military men take risks, but they never gamble. Being audacious and daring is a desirable martial characteristic and a quality military instructors the world over encourage their students to exercise while at the same time warning about gambling. Taking a risk is only ever done after a careful estimation of the situation, when one's alternative courses of actions are considered and contrasted; and a measured assessment of the options selected are weighted by criteria, often mathematically scored. The gamble is a more reckless, 'devil may care', exposure to hazard. Napoleon gambled that he had judged the underlying mood of the French people and army correctly, that their level of dissatisfaction with the restored

Bourbon Monarchy was such that if he presented himself, they would follow him. Uncertain as this was, and it was indeterminable, a far greater unknown would be the reaction in capitals across Europe. He gambled that the unity of effort continuing in Vienna was more apparent than real, a façade that would crack. In the event, his reappearance galvanised it! Europe was alarmed, France's Bourbon Monarch Louis XVIII was amazed, Marshal Soult was put in charge of the defences around Paris, while Marshal Ney was dispatched south from the French capital, boastfully declaring he would bring Napoleon back to Paris 'in an iron cage'. Shortly after, Wellington learned of Napoleon's sudden arrival onto French soil in Provence where he and his few followers were confronted by Marshal Ney with the 5th Regiment. While both sides, with weapons ready, sized up the tense moment, Napoleon seized it with typical bravado, flung open his greatcoat and with both hands brought up to his chest invited the Bourbon troops 'to fire upon your Emperor'. Despite being ordered to do so, none did, and they joined him, as later did the 7th Regiment at Grenoble. All the way to Paris it was the same. His first gamble was over, causing him to remark, 'Before Grenoble, I was an adventurer, after Grenoble I was a Prince'. If, in the case of the former gamble he proved himself correct, in the latter he had miscalculated. Even before Napoleon reached Paris, the rest of Europe had branded him 'an enemy of humanity', and all Europe declared war against him. Napoleon's escape from Elba and likely restoration of the Empire could not be tolerated by the Allies, who sought to crush this emergent threat to European peace. However, as far as Napoleon was concerned, 'he who saves a nation, violates no law'.

Napoleon had now to gamble a third time, and at its essence was time. He needed time to consolidate in order to regenerate a war-weary army and population, tired of bloodshed, conscription and

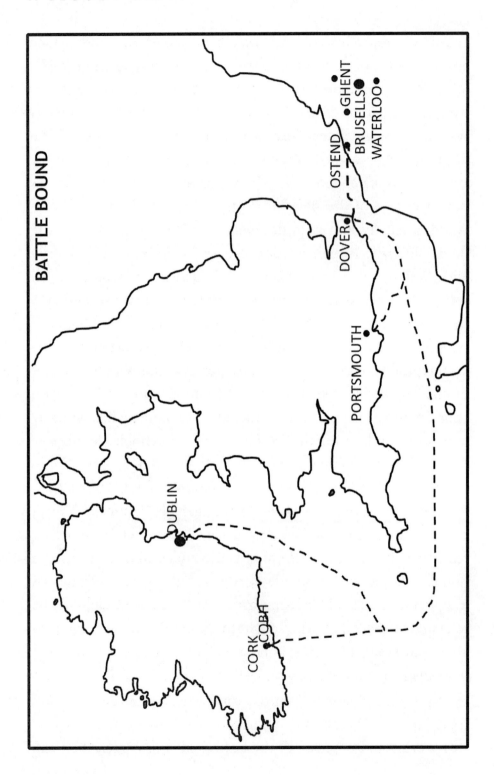

BATTLE BOUND

OSTEND
GHENT
BRUSELLS
WATERLOO
DOVER
PORTSMOUTH
DUBLIN
CORK
COBH

taxes. He needed time to recruit, rearm, reconfigure. He needed time to prepare for war. This time too, he knew only too well, would be usefully used by his opponents, Austria, Russia, Prussia, and Britain. They could mobilise huge armies in excess of anything France could muster; 650,000 troops were converging on France – the noose was tightening. He faced a stark choice, to wait and grow a large force to defend French territory, or strike early and take a less large French force on a pre-emptive offensive to isolate the earlier mobilising Anglo-Allied (British, Dutch, German, and Belgian) and Prussian armies, and annihilate each one separately before the massive Austrian and Russian armies, taking longer to mobilise, could arrive. In doing so, the vast superiority in numbers of the European coalition would be greatly diminished. He would then seek the possibility of peace with Austria and Russia. Napoleon chose to use less time and undertake an audacious grand gamble. All this caused Tsar Alexander I of Russia to remark to Wellington, mindful of his recent successfully concluded seven-year campaign against Napoleon's generals on the Iberian Peninsula, 'It is for you to save the world again.'

Bound for Battle

The sight and sound of soldiers marching in unison will always guarantee the rapt attention of those standing close by, and this early May morning in 1815 Dublin was no exception as the men of the 28th (North Gloucestershire) Regiment of Foot stretched along a good length of the Liffey quaysides. 'It's the Slashers, it's the Slashers' came the cry. The 28th Foot were so-called for their purposeful use of the sword in the early part of the 1812 American War. Those who looked on were mesmerised by the movement of the many as one, the regularity of the marching pace, the instantaneous exactness of response to bawled orders. As always, the discipline and seriousness were palpable but what was also mesmerising was the evident absence of anxiety, replaced ironically by an almost casual concentration that only comes from perhaps hundreds of hours of repeated drilling on barrack squares.

Forming lines from close column, retreating in line only to then advance 100 paces, going from hollow squares into line again, this time four ranks deep instead of two – these and more were all sequences intended to encompass much of what would be required on the battlefield, the fundamental order of infantry, a uniform system of manoeuvre. They were written in a manual some 27 years previously in 1788 by 'Old Pivot', General Sir David Dundas, when stationed in Dublin. Known as *Dundas's Principles of Military Movement*, this manual became mandatory when an amended version was officially issued four years later in June 1792 as *Rules and Regulations for the Movement of his Majesty's Infantry* by the Adjutant General, William Fawcett. This unified system of drill formed the basis of British infantry tactics in the Napoleonic Wars (1803-1814) and was again to be utilized by the 28th Foot and other British infantry regiments at Waterloo.

Unknown to the assembled on-lookers and admirers, 'the Slashers' ought not in fact to have been marching down along Dublin's quayside that May morning, as they had previously sailed from Cork on a transatlantic journey some four months previously. Unfavourable winds, however, made them return to the port of 'Cove' (Cobh or, Queenstown) and kept them ashore until mid-March. With the clearing of the adverse weather, they set sail once more, their second attempt no more successful than their first, a storm making them seek safe refuge back in harbour the same night. With the war against the 'Yankees' ending, their presence in North America was deemed redundant and they were sent to the north of Ireland, only then to learn the dramatic news of Napoleon's escape from Elba and his bold bid for Empire once more. The 28th Foot were one of twelve veteran Peninsular War infantry battalions to now be heading for Belgium, this time embarked from Dublin.

Belgium, as we know it today, was then in fact part of the new part-French, part-Dutch Kingdom of the Netherlands, lying to the north of France. British regiments were making for it in haste from America, Ireland, England, and elsewhere. Not all would make it on time. Wellington would dearly have loved to have with him, as the core of his army, the bulk of those troops who had served with him in the Peninsula. In the event, he had to do with only part of that army. Apart from the King's German Legion (KGL) and a few other exceptions, Wellington did not hold the remainder of his allies, Dutch and Belgians mostly, in terribly high regard due to their uncertain quality and lack of experience, many young and untried. This is what he meant when he spoke of his Waterloo army as being 'infamous'. This Anglo-Dutch or, Anglo-Allied Army was to link with the Prussians and together advance from Belgium (The Netherlands) and fight Napoleon on French soil. This army was forming up, and converging on Belgium were British regiments at different stages of preparedness, the 28th Foot amongst them. Among the ranks of the 28th were the newcomers, freshly recruited in Ireland, along with the more seasoned experienced Peninsular War veterans and the old campaigners.

Among the officers of the 28th were a number from Ireland, including their second-in-command, Major Robert Nixon of Mullynesker, son of Alexander Nixon, the High Sheriff of Fermanagh. He had seen previous service in Egypt and the Peninsula and was to assume command of the 28th on the wounding of its commander. Also there was Captain Richard Kelly from Galway, who likewise took command after the wounding of Major Nixon, until he too was wounded. He had a brother, Major T.E. Kelly, who fought

The Duke of Wellington (The National Gallery of Ireland).

at Waterloo with the 95th Rifles. There was a Captain Thomas English from Armagh, who had prior service in the Peninsula and was to be wounded at Waterloo. There was also a Captain Charles Peter Teulon from Bandon, County Cork. Lieutenant John Wellington Shelton, heir of John Shelton of Rossmore House, Limerick, had also served in the Peninsula and was to be four times wounded at Waterloo. Lieutenant Robert Prescott Eason, from a well to do family in Cork City, had served in the Peninsular War and had distinguished himself at the Passage of the Douro. He had received a number of wounds in the course of the war and was again wounded at Waterloo. One of these wounds was to the head, and in the 1830s as an in-mate of the Royal Hospital Kilmainham, Dublin, symptoms were to resurface and cause him difficulties.

With the rest of the 28th Foot they all began boarding the transport ships from the stonewalled quays of the River Liffey next to Dublin's Carlisle (now O'Connell) Bridge. From the bridge's parapet, the onlookers had a perfect view of the scene, a 'live' embarkation in progress, a regiment going to war. With a sense of horror they witnessed an older soldier who was stumbling along a gangplank fall into the murky, cold waters of the Liffey. His body would not surface until much later; the first casualty of the hundred days' conflict that would follow had been recorded.

Inescapably Irish

Wellington, whether he did or did not like being referred to as an Irishman, was inescapably Irish. Born in Dublin in 1769, Arthur was the third (surviving) son of Garret Wesely, first Earl of Mornington, Trim, County Meath. In 1798, subject to the provision of receipt of an inheritance, the family changed the spelling to Wellesly, an earlier form. His father was a prominent Anglo-Irish peer, fathering five sons and one daughter. Wellington's family heritage was Irish for some six centuries. Descended from an Anglo-Norman family that had settled in Ireland in the 12th century, his ancestors had abandoned Catholicism for the Anglican religion in order to regain their sequestered lands. Few Ascendancy families were totally isolated, and many had a mixture of Gaelic, Norman, and English descent. He spent his early years in Ireland between two houses, Dangan Castle, three miles north of Summerhill on the Trim road in County Meath, and one on Merrion Street, Dublin. He was educated both in Trim and in Dublin. A downturn in the family's finances, his father having overspent on lavish parties and continual ornamental improvements to his estate, required a move to Chelsea in London where the living conditions were cheaper. After his father's sudden death, the eldest son, Richard, took matters in hand and began to attempt to restore an order to their affairs, whereupon Arthur, a quiet, lonely boy, spent two unhappy years in Eaton before the family relocated in Brussels. Now 16, he was regarded by his somewhat despairing mother as ungainly and uncomfortable in company, with little evident academic leanings, and she decided to send her 'ugly boy Arthur' to a military academy at Angers in France to learn a useful trade. Arthur acquired French with a good accent along with a new-found interest and a self-confidence. Commissioned first into a Highland Regiment, his brother Richard then secured an appointment for him as aide-de-camp to the Lord Lieutenant of Ireland, and so Arthur returned to Ireland and soon also became a sitting MP for Trim in the Irish Parliament.

The so-called Ascendancy contained elements of all ethnic groups, and it is not possible to isolate a distinct 'Anglo-Irish' class. The Ascendancy was simply the class that owned the land and ran the country by a mixture of means, regardless of the ethnic or religious mix in their make-up and background, though the majority were Anglican Protestant. As opposed to how nationality is understood more strictly now, those of that class could then consider themselves, and did, to be both Irish and British at the one time. The often quoted remark of Wellington disowning his Irishness – that 'just because you were born in a stable does not necessarily make you a horse'– is neither definitively attributable to him to nor is the context in which it was supposedly said understood. The words may have been uttered by him in a discussion in which someone made a remark about a particular Irish unit having a reputation for heavy drinking, when he wished to distance himself from this, meaning that because he too was Irish did not necessarily make him a heavy drinker. He was equally attributed with the remark that 'the Battle of Waterloo was won on the playing fields of Eaton', a school and a time of his life of which he did not have happy memories. There is little likelihood that Wellington ever uttered either remark, and every likelihood that he uttered neither.

Wellington's Irishness is not in question. It could not have been then, as it cannot be now. He would have known this at the time, and he would not have seen his Irishness as mutually exclusive to his Englishness. He would have regarded himself as both, something that was commonly understood by the Ascendancy class of the time. To a large extent the Anglo-Irish officer class regarded themselves, and in turn were regarded, as Irish, British, or English simultaneously. They were not obliged to choose between identities. If they chose to ignore any aspect of their simultaneous identities, it is doubtful that they could have actually achieved that, as this is simply how they were regarded. Wellington had an inescapable identity, and this inherited identity was inescapably Irish.

'Clockwork Musketry'

Fire-power was the most decisive factor on the battlefield, and whoever brought the most of it to bear invariably won. More precisely, it was the effect that massed, well-packed lines of infantry produced by steadily delivering a constant out-pouring of volley fire that mattered. In short, it was its 'stopping power' that was important. The Battle of Waterloo was a specific instance of this. Napoleon wanted to destroy Wellington's army, which, to survive, had to stand its ground unflinchingly. Waterloo was where Wellington's cautious but courageous defensive posture was to be pitted against Napoleon's offensive manoeuvring élan and verve.

Fighting formation brought fire-power to bear. The singular soldier, a trained man with his muzzle-loaded, smooth-bore flintlock 'Brown Bess' musket, was virtually useless alone, but with others could be highly effective.. The rate of fire, range, and accuracy determined the musket's effect. These were slow, short, and inaccurate, respectively. Combined, however, cool continuous discharged volumes of volley fire in groups could be harnessed to give deadly effect, especially if fire was held until the enemy had closed to within 50 yards or less.

To achieve the effective use of all available muskets, or the greater part thereof, a defensive formation appropriate to the circumstances combined with steadiness in the ranks was key. Individual mastery of weapon handling was crucial and it was here the highly trained British soldier had earned a reputation for a steady, well-practised proficiency. The 'Brown Bess' had a barrel length of 39 inches and weighed slightly in excess of nine pounds. To achieve a high rate of fire, three rounds per minute, without wavering, the soldier had to be highly trained, well drilled, and disciplined. The 'Brown Bess' or 'Indian Pattern', being a muzzle-loaded weapon, required the soldier to stand up to do so and since it was a flintlock, the mechanics of firing were somewhat involved. Suffice to say that loading, aiming, and firing was a complicated process, requiring 20 individual movements to fire each round. The overall objective was to achieve three rounds per minute or 20 seconds per round, thus allowing one second per movement – and all the while the enemy approaching or even firing at you. Reliable infantry in separate entities of a cohesive whole were trained to fire at the same moment, or to provide a continuous running volley, the entire formation delivering their murderous execution by maintaining a steadiness in the ranks and a consistency in volume. To achieve this effect in battle, well-trained infantry needed to be well led. At the time, officers in the British army received their commissions by purchase, while advancement was secured by payment, seniority, or patronage. A vacancy had to exist and he who sought it had to have money to buy it. Merit or talent had little bearing on the matter. The sons of landed gentry provided their fair share of officers to the army and navy, and these 'gentlemen' were literate, could ride and shoot, and possessed a natural authoritative air and an innate sense of fairness. So the system, worked. The aristocracy, contrary to popular belief, was by no means all-pervasive among the officer ranks, which also included the sons of professionals, 'gentlemen in trade', smaller landowners and farmers, and, of course sons of serving or retired officers. Land, wealth, and education, all together or separately, were the all-important qualifications, and of them all the ability to read and write proved the great social divider.

Fire-power was, of course, also provided by artillery, and Wellington kept a tight tactical control over his gunners. The Royal Engineers and the Royal Artillery trained their officers before giving them commissions, and only on passing their exams. A rigid adherence to seniority meant promotion was slow and would have been more so had it not expanded threefold between 1791 and 1814 (274 to 727 officers), and the Royal Military Academy at Woolwich, established in 1741, was hard put to keep pace with the call for officers. The Royal Artillery, although deployed all over the world, was nonetheless much centralised at Woolwich. A close-knit grouping, they shared a strong, proud ethos, and it was a family affair. Many were the sons of gunner officers, and there was much inter-marriage with sisters and daughters of fellow gunner officers. The 12th century St Nicholas Plumstead parish church near Woolwich in Kent was situated in open space on ground that sloped gently to the Thames River. It was here on the 16 May 1815, that Second Lieutenant William Harrison Harvey, Royal Artillery, second son of John Harvey, a member of the legal profession who had a reasonable size estate at Mount Pleasant, County Wexford, married Elisabeth Mary Colebrooke of Barn Cottage in Eltham near London. Elizabeth was the daughter of Colonel Paulet Colebrooke (Royal Artillery) and his wife Elizabeth Jane. Colonel Paulet Colebrooke returned from a tour of duty in Ceylon in 1815 and died in 1816. He had a son, William Macbean George Colebrooke, who served in the Royal Artillery and who became a career diplomat after his service. William Harrison Harvey served in Major William Lloyd's Brigade of the Royal Artillery at Waterloo where he lost an arm. His wedding day was also the day he left for Belgium, and before leaving he and his new wife Elizabeth longingly embraced; it would be the first and last time Elizabeth would feel both her husband's arms around her. William's father John was a first cousin of Beauchamp Bagenal Harvey who led the 1798 rebellion in Wexford. William's brother was named George Washington Harvey, his father demonstrating his anti-British politics in so naming him. George Washington Harvey and another brother had both died separately in 1813 while serving with the Royal Navy. John Harvey had married Mary Harrison (William Harvey's mother), the daughter of William Harrison of Castle Harrison near Charleville in County Cork. Mary Harrison's brother William was married to Margaret O'Grady, a daughter of

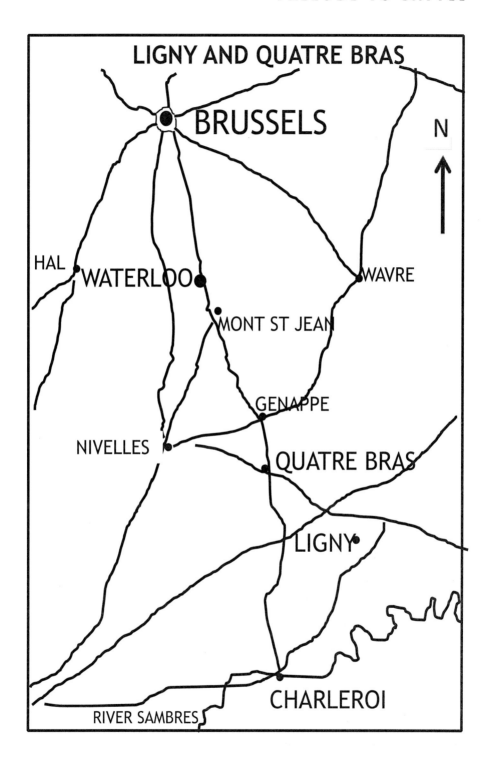

Standish O'Grady who was the prosecutor of Robert Emmet in 1803. William Harrison had fought with the Austrian army against Napoleon until 1793.

All of this demonstrates a not untypical instance of the web of connectivity between families, their inter-marriage, and seemingly contradictory sympathies arising from Ireland's past history. This inter-relationship of the 'Irish' with different and sometimes differing perspectives on matters reveals the complicated allegiances and confusing and confused loyalties of the Anglo-Irish gentry of those times. Much of these, however, were very much aligned in opposing Napoleon's latest belligerent advances into Europe. He had to be stopped, and it was only fire-power that would do so.

'Humbugged'

The town of Charleroi, where Wellington had not expected Napoleon to cross the French frontier into Belgium was exactly where he did so with more than 120,000 men of his Armée du Nord. Napoleon had again executed his 'strategy of the central position', striking hard and fast, using surprise, speed, and security to come between the forces of a larger foe. To turn numerical disadvantage to advantage by driving a wedge between both of his opponent's halves, then attacking and defeating each separately – '*divide et impera*' (divide and conquer) – was Napoleon's tactic, using just enough force to hold one in place while concentrating the majority of his own force to defeat the second. He did not have to destroy it completely, just to destroy any hope of it assisting the other. He would then turn to demolish the part of his opponent's army he had previously fixed in place. The combination of Wellington's Anglo-Allied army, more than 74,000 men (British, Dutch, Belgians, and Germans) and Blücher's 100,000 Prussians was simply too big for Napoleon to defeat. His best defence was a sudden, sharp offensive.

If he could come between them, first fight one, then the other, he might succeed in sending the Prussians east, back across the Rhine, and subsequently drive Wellington north-west, back along his line of communications towards Ostend, leaving Brussels open to him. By striking direct for Brussels, dividing Wellington and Blücher, getting between them and keeping them apart, this might of itself send them back along the separate ways they came, and the Belgian capital would be in French hands and a psychological victory achieved. Napoleon might then be able to negotiate with Austria and Russia who were busily mobilising huge armies in excess of 150,000 men each, and salvage a peace deal, restoring pride for France – perhaps later, to restore the previous extent of the former French Empire.

Wellington's confidence in his spy network had been misplaced. He had, of course, received reports from the field of French troops mobilising and concentrating across the frontier in France, but he was unsure if this was a deliberate feint and that Napoleon's real point of attack would be executed elsewhere. He did not wish to commit his troops too early and to the wrong place, incorrectly falling for a deception and allowing Napoleon to manoeuvre around him. He waited for his secret network of information gatherers to confirm or otherwise illuminate him. He received neither, only silence. Wellington's intelligence failure had left him blind, and he was caught out, leading him to remark, 'Napoleon has humbugged me, by God'. He had now to get his army to a speedily selected delaying position at the crossroads of Quatre Bras. Napoleon was on the move, and speedily so; he had gained the initiative, and his advance needed to be stalled, so Wellington and Blücher could reconfigure and combine. Napoleon had put them off balance and he intended capitalizing on this and was moving at pace.

Gaining Impetus

Surprise achieved, his momentous momentum maintained, Napoleon intended to continue the impetus of his forces' advance by high tempo movement. To ensure the rapidity of this propulsion he dispatched Marshal Ney with a force to occupy the vital position of Quatre Bras from which, having pounded the Prussians into submission at Ligny, he would use the crucial crossroads as a pivot or springboard to then crush Wellington, his Anglo-Allied army fixed into an unfavoured position by Marshal Ney.

Napoleon did successfully maul Blücher and his Prussians, who had over-extended themselves along marshy ground, suffering 20,000 casualties for the loss of 14,000 French, which Napoleon could ill-afford. Nonetheless the Prussians were in retreat and Napoleon sent Marshal Grouchy with more than 30,000 men in pursuit to ensure they did not join with Wellington. Napoleon, having achieved the first part of his plan, hurried to Quatre Bras to execute the second part.

In less than his customary dynamic fashion, Marshal Ney displayed a peculiar absence of energy and lapse of judgement in not initially seizing Quatre Bras. His delaying allowed Wellington to arrive, hold off Ney's subsequent attacks, and consequently, on hearing of Blücher's defeat, to withdraw in good order. Ney further compounded his errors by not continuing to harass or pursue Wellington in retreat. On arrival at Quatre Bras, an incredulous Napoleon was furious; all that he had won at Ligny was lost at Quatre Bras and with it time, time for Wellington to choose his ground, to be better prepared for the next round of fighting, if there was to be such. The opportunity for Napoleon to engage Wellington on his own in a rushed tempo on unfavourable ground had been lost. He wasn't sure if he would get another.

It was now a matter of direction. Along which route would Blücher and his defeated Prussians retreat? Which way would he withdraw? East, back across the Rhine or north towards Brussels ? Away from or towards Wellington? To stay separated from or to combine with Wellington? Without Blücher and his Prussians, Wellington was unlikely to engage, let alone defeat Napoleon and might well abandon Brussels and seek advantage further back along his line of communications towards the coast. Blücher had Marshal Grouchy and 30,000 Frenchmen on his trail, and was advised by his chief of staff, who was distrustful of Wellington, to go east, but Blücher, who hated the French, marched north to support Wellington as he had promised.

Dramatic as Napoleon's surprise strike into Belgium and successful separation of the Anglo-Allied army was, exciting as the concurrent battles at Ligny and Quatre Bras were, and sensational as Blücher's decision to keep to his promise with Wellington was, matters were to become even more spectacularly electrifying. It was all only a prelude to something that would burn the name Waterloo into the minds of men for ever.

Turbulence

Wet and weary soldiers awoke on the sodden, waterlogged Waterloo terrain. The unrelenting rain of a summer thunderstorm had turned much of the surface, a loamy rich soil, to mud, through which infantry and cavalry would now have to trudge and into which artillery would sink. The French had fought with mud on their boots before, it was not going to stop them, but the ill effects of the previous night's atrocious weather had made the most ordinary tasks more maddeningly troublesome and, importantly, made difficult the concentration of Napoleon's grand artillery battery. The overnight torrential downpour had initially impeded movement, marring manoeuvrability, and so delayed the battle's beginning.

Delayed also was Lieutenant Colonel John Dawson, 2nd Earl of Portarlington from Emo Court, County Laois. An experienced officer, he had seen service in the Peninsular War and in June 1815 he was officer commanding the 23rd Regiment of Light Dragoons. At the battle's commencement on the morning of 18 June he was not where his duty required him to be, present with his regiment. The reason for this has never been confirmed and versions vary – taken ill, his servant neglected to wake him, he had on the previous evening departed to Brussels to seek enjoyment. Whatever account is correct, the essential truth is he was not at Waterloo commanding his regiment as the battle got under way. He did return to find the fighting well progressed and his regiment already decisively engaged. Eager to compensate for his absence, he attached himself to the 18th Hussars and fought with commendable courage for what remained of the day, having a horse shot from under him near the height of hostilities, but it was insufficient to redeem him, more especially in his own eyes, and the episode severely damaged his standing. His absence from duty on such an occasion required his retirement from the 23rd Regiment of Light Dragoons in September 1815. Although receiving much support from the not insufficient patronage of no less a person than the Prince Regent himself who did his best to uphold the unfortunate officer, as no one who knew him doubted his courage, he felt he was unable to escape the supposedly dishonourably viewed action unbecoming of an officer commanding. He allowed this unfortunate incident to mar his future, and he squandered the remainder of his life, wasting a large fortune and any hope of redemption. He died unmarried in a boarding house in an obscure London slum in late December 1845. That then was his singular future fate; for now, on the eve of battle, all those present had to cope with the severe torrential rain. Captain (later Colonel) George Cotter, second son of the Reverend George Sackville Cotter from Youghal, County Cork, was to recollect that,

> the night was so cold and the rain of the previous day had been so heavy, that the surface of the whole ridge upon which we lay was quickly converted into thin mud, through which we sank more than ankle deep. I preferred standing up and walking to and fro during the hours of darkness to lying upon such a bed. The night wore tediously away, and frequently during the late hours, while the sounds from either army met my ears, did I repeat the lines in which Shakespeare depicts the rival camps during the night before the battle of Agincourt.

Most of the day before the battle had been marked by appalling weather. This pouring rain did, however, do much to assist in covering the withdrawal of Wellington's army north to the Waterloo position as they were harassed and harried by the French. To counter this pressure, an element of Wellington's army were 'left in contact' to delay and hamper the French, and such rearguard action saw exchanges between the respective cavalries charging and counter-charging. Lieutenant Standish Darby O'Grady, 2nd Viscount Guillamore, 7th Hussars, from County Limerick, gave a description of one such encounter in a letter to his Father:

> We charged the Head of their whole cavalry – Their front were Lancers – their flanks were protected for they were in the street and the mass of cavalry in the rear were so great that I defy them to go about. We killed the officer who was in front but we could not reach the men as the lancers of the front and rear kept the men at bay.[Afterwards] the French pursued us nearly ¾ of a mile in which they were charged repeatedly by the other squadron of the 7th, but they were too strong for us; we however killed a great many and got out of the road at last.

Repulsed, the 7th Hussars did manage to get clear due to a series of successful support charges by the 1st Life Guards. One such tussle amongst the many fleeting fracases saw Captain Edward Kelly from Portarlington, County Laois, lead a successful foray with the 1st Life Guards. Along with the 7th Hussars, 1st Life Guards, and the heavy cavalry of the Royal Horse Guards (the 'Oxford Blues'), the 23rd Light Dragoons, were the Royal Horse Artillery and the 95th Rifles, all forming the rearguard. Under the overall command of the cavalry corps commander, Lieutenant General the Earl of Uxbridge, their task was to see Wellington's main body withdraw unmolested, marching off from Quatre Bras up the single high road in the direction of Brussels to Mont-St-Jean and Waterloo. The rearguard had to fight a series of skirmishes with the French but without allowing itself to become seriously attacked. This skilful bit of skulduggery also involved giving the impression that Wellington's entire army was present, and partaking in the hustle, bustle, and tussle. Having successfully kept the French at bay, the rearguard disengaged and joined the northward movement but artillery exchanges continued. Had anyone glanced skywards, an ominous towering cloud formation was becoming evident from the north, the air cooling as it rose and water vapour condensed and formed great cumulus clouds. These building clouds were made entirely of water. The cumulus tops were crisp and well-defined, looking much like a cauliflower, and were an unmissable indication of developing atmospheric instability. The basic ingredients of a summer thunderstorm, moisture lift and instability, were brewing. Over several hours of uplifts and downlifts, a latent heat or energy in the form of a natural electricity was released and flashes of bright light were produced, this lightening followed by the crashing noise of thunder. The sky turned a purple-black and inevitably there came a point when the updraught ceased, dominated by the downdraught, and the suspended condensation, water droplets high in the clouds, fell to the ground in an unceasing heavy rain, then as a torrential downpour. A particularly severe storm raged through the night of June 17, a loud, confused commotion of tumultuous rain, thunder claps, and thunderbolts.

If the heavens were disturbed they would soon to be matched by earthly turbulence and the flow of human blood. Across a large part of Belgium, columns of troops, cannons, and cavalry were all in purposeful motion, Wellington north to Waterloo, with Napoleon and Marshal Ney not far behind, Blücher north to Waterloo via Weave with Marshal Grouchy in loose pursuit, and British units force-marching south from Belgian ports. That much movement was afoot was sure, but there was also much that was equally unsure: for instance, Napoleon did not know if Wellington would stand and actually fight at Waterloo; neither did Napoleon know that Marshal Grouchy was unaware where Blücher and his Prussians actually were, and Wellington did not know if Blücher, in the renewed circumstances after Ligny and Quatre Bras, would commit to stand with him at Waterloo. To each was unknown a part of the picture that would soon fill the frame of what was to become the Battle of Waterloo.

Retreating in step

The thunderstorm and downpour meant there was no escape from the darkness, cold and hunger that night, and all this after miles and miles, days and days of hard marching, counter-marching, little sleep, scant rations, and scarce creature comforts. The only possible consolation each side could take from the situation was that it applied equally to all in the three armies, Wellington's, Napoleon's and Blücher's respectively. In addition, many were not long recovered from the battles at Ligny and Quatre Bras. In the second of these, fewer than

10,000 Allied troops, mostly Dutch, initially faced Marshal Ney's superior force, the imbalance only being adjusted with the late but timely arrival of Wellington and General Picton's British forces. No longer outnumbered, having 30,000 men and 70 guns, they repelled repeated French cavalry charges; these were largely unsupported by French infantry and were repulsed by the infantry forming squares and the effective quick deployment of artillery. The strategically important crossroads was held by the Allies, and Marshal Ney was prevented from seizing it, thus denying the decisive dividing of the Anglo-Allied army from the Prussians. The battle itself ended in a tactical stalemate, with losses to British, Allied, and French strengths, but significantly Marshal Ney had let a golden opportunity slip by when circumstances were favourable to him. Napoleon was unable to capitalise on his defeat of the Prussians at the concurrently fought Battle of Ligny, and his preferred rate of advance towards Brussels had been frustrated. Wellington had bought important time to pick the ground of his choosing on which to place a defence if he could convince Blücher and his Prussians to stand with him. For now they would both retreat in step, their forces largely intact.

Even though Wellington's soldiers had not lost the Battle of Quatre Bras, they nonetheless found themselves in retreat and were now perched on the ridge of Mont-St-Jean, soaked to the skin, hungry, tired, in darkness, and not knowing if tomorrow they would continue the withdrawal or stand and fight. Many were physically degraded, exhausted, some shocked. Seven of Wellington's non-Peninsular regiments had just fought at Quatre Bras, and three of his heretofore unbloodied units suffered heavily. They were glad of the respite to rest and reflect on their experiences, but the elements were granting little relief.

Private Edward Costello, 95th Rifles, from County Laois was trying to come to terms with an incident he had witnessed during the rearguard's withdrawal from Quatre Bras. Some of the women who accompanied the soldiers to Brussels had ventured south with their men. A battalion had a paper strength of ten companies, a hundred soldiers in each. Men were actively discouraged from marrying and only six per company were officially granted permission to allow their wives accompany them on campaign. Officially they were placed on half rations and would perhaps tailor and wash uniforms for the soldiers of the company in return. Unofficially, other wives went abroad with their husbands. In the aftermath of Quatre Bras, Private Costello was on a track which,

> was partially protected by a hedge from the enemy's fire, when one of my companions heard the cries of a child on the other side; on looking over he espied a fine boy, about two or three years of age, by the side of its dead mother, who was still bleeding copiously from a wound in the head, occasioned, most likely, by a random shot from the enemy. We carried the motherless, and perhaps orphan child by turns to Genappe, where we found a number of women of our division, one of whom recognised the little fellow, I think she said as belonging to a soldier of the First Royals.

Similarly, Irishman Captain Harry Ross-Lewin had noted the presence within the battalion, the 32nd Foot, whose rank and file consisted of 38 per cent Irishmen, of at least four other Irish officers: his younger brother Thomas, who was a lieutenant, as well as a trio of captains, Jaques Boyse (Boyce), Thomas Cassen, and Edward Whitty. In what Ross-Lewin remembered as a 'rather singular' occurrence, all three Irish captains died as a result of wounds received during Quatre Bras. He had, of course, omitted Lieutenant Samuel Hill Lawrence of Cork, whose son would earn a Victoria Cross in 1857 for his gallantry with the 32nd Foot during the Indian Mutiny.

Private Costello, Captain Ross-Lewin, and doubtlessly others were thoughtful of these events and wary of what was likely to follow.

Others undoubtedly were anxious for action. They were soldiers, had been for years, and this was their life. Paradoxically, the army offered them security and stability along with boredom and discomfort, and all for a shilling a day minus deductions for 'necessaries', food and other basics. When campaigning they were given raw rations which they had to cook themselves. There were slight margins between life's on-going hardships inside and outside the army, and many were motivated to join by economic circumstance, others by the lure and attraction of military life itself, some seeking travel and adventure. In or out of uniform, they were human and for all the 'bluster for battle' and a certain fatalism, the survival instinct was, as always, strong. No one wanted to die, least of all violently, suffering perhaps a horrible death, maybe even after a lingering period of agonising pain, or else, shockingly instantaneous. At Quatre Bras they had witnessed comrades, friends, maybe family, brothers, father, sons, cousins, killed and wounded. They had experienced fear and the distress of uncertainty. This, and more besides, was not something that soldiers ever got inured to by a supposed 'battle-hardness', rather it was an acclimatisation to this gruesome reality simply being no longer new, yet the ghastly effects were still no less felt. This cumulative familiarity with such harrowing experiences was no barrier insulating them from the nerve-racking actuality of life cut savagely short or exposure to extreme harm. They appreciated that it was a diabolical waste of human life, endeavour, and resources. They knew that the price of freedom was eternal vigilance and the price for peace was war. The Battle of Waterloo was about to extract a very heavy levy indeed.

Major Arthur Heyland, 40th Foot, from County Derry, no doubt wondering if he would be among those paying this price, engaged himself in writing a letter to his wife, to be delivered in the event of his death:

> My Mary, let the recollection console you that the happiest days of my life have been from your love and affection and that I die loving only you, and with a fervent hope that our souls may be reunited hereafter and part no more.
>
> What dear children, my Mary, I leave you. My Marianna, gentlest girl, may God bless you. My Anne, my John, may Heaven protect you. My children may you all be happy and may the reflection that your father never in life swerved from the truth and always acted from the dictates of his conscience, preserve you, virtuous and happy, for without virtue there can be no happiness.
>
> My darling Mary I must tell you again how tranquilly I shall die, should it be my fate to fall, we cannot, my own love, die together – one or other must witness the loss of what we love must. Let my children console you, my love, my Mary.

Stand up and fight

Countryside is scenery until you place a soldier on it, then suddenly it becomes terrain. Landscape is admired, terrain is analysed. Natural features are viewed with regard to how they might be made the most of for military purposes. To do so, the military mind conducts a ground appreciation. Before maximising what an area of the earth's solid surface may have to offer, other considerations are simultaneously taken into account: the state of one's own and enemy forces; the commander's intent; the time and space available; and the overall tactical and strategic objective. A landscape may include a hill, in military terms high ground. This key terrain grants an advantage, the putting of one's own forces on a higher level in a comparatively favourable position, and as such is a critical asset to have and to hold. The enemy are disadvantaged by the increased arduousness of having to attack up-hill, the steepness of the gradient of its forward slope making progress difficult and tiring, hindering their movement. The open ground in front at its base, stretching outwards, offers good observation and fields of fire for those defending – in short, a 'killing ground' for artillery fire. Equally, for those advancing onto the raised ground, the low-lying area in front may offer unobstructed avenues of approach. Folds and creases, undulations and the otherwise wave-like shape of the terrain's surface, buildings, road networks, rivers, streams, trees and hedges, alternatively provide cover and concealment for the skilful manoeuvring of troops on either flank, or equally proving disadvantageous as obstacles to be negotiated. The physical nature of the terrain to be fought on dictates the tactical options available to both defenders and attackers, those who employ them to best advantage benefiting accordingly. Napoleon was the master of the offensive manoeuvre, Wellington talented in defence. Their use of ground and their potent combinations of infantry, artillery, and cavalry assets in tandem with orchestrated timing made them masters of the battlefield. Leadership is about effectiveness, and in this regard both were unsurpassed. Wellington's choice of defensive lines were highly considered; he favoured employing the protection offered by the occupying the reserve slope of hills – positioning his troops neither on the forward slope nor crest of the high ground, rather beyond on the key terrain's far or unseen side, behind the hilltop itself and so hidden from view, shielded from cannon fire. Wellington had employed this 'reverse slope' tactic to very good effect during his involvements in the Peninsular War. His generals, commanders, and troops understood how he wished it to be employed and had done so successfully throughout. He could not, however, win battles by this alone, but had to make it work by combining this posture with a number of other factors, foremost among which was the cool, steady, disciplined delivery of what Wellington referred to as 'clockwork volleys' of musketry fire-power, at which the British army excelled. In the event on Sunday 18 June 1815, Wellington conducted an apparent 'hasty defence' on what was believed to be randomly selected ground after a day-long fighting retreat throughout the 17th, having previously engaged the French in the not inconsiderable battle at the delaying position at Quatre Bras on the 16th. Simultaneously, the Prussians under their legendary 73-year-old beloved commander, Field Marshal Prince Gebhard von Blücher, nicknamed 'Alte Forwarts' (Always Forward), fought the bigger battle at Ligny and lost. Napoleon had hoped the matter could be decided at Ligny with either of his generals Ney or D'Erlon delivering the fatal blow by attacking the Prussian right flank. Meanwhile Blücher had hoped the matter could be decided at Ligny also, but by Wellington delivering the fatal blow by attacking the French left flank. Neither had happened, the matter remaining undecided. Now, Wellington was hoping the matter could be decisively decided at Waterloo by Blücher attacking the French right flank. For his part he had to occupy and hold his selected position until Blücher came to his aid, the combined strength of Wellington and Blücher together being too much for Napoleon. For that to happen, both Blücher and Wellington would have firstly to retreat separately, but 'in step', in what in today's terminology would be called the conducting of 'retrograde operations', where space on the ground is traded for time – time, that is, for both Blücher and Wellington's armies to get 'in line' together. The Battle of Waterloo, its success or failure, involved many factors, not least amongst them the dimensions of space and time. Could they succeed in combining their forces in the one place at the one time to combat Napoleon? Wellington knew of the place, and therefore it became a matter of time, but would or could Blücher reach Waterloo in time? Wellington, amazingly, knew of Waterloo; he had a year previously reconnoitred the area and conducted a thorough, unhurried and fulsome ground appreciation. He had viewed the area's natural features with a mind as to how they might be made the most of for military purposes. He identified the key terrain, the cover and concealment, the avenue of approach, and the obstacles. He had stood along the ridge of Mont-St-Jean and 'looked out'; importantly he also viewed the area from the opposite ridge of La Belle Alliance, two thirds of a mile away, and 'looked in' across the shallow valley and received the attacker's perspective of the ground. All this he had kept in his pocket should it ever, however unlikely, come to pass that he needed this knowledge, and, astonishingly, it did! He chose there, in the unusual circumstance he found himself, as the site to place his 'deliberate defence'. Its extraordinariness lay in its ordinariness. What was remarkable about Waterloo, that shallow valley near Braine l'Alleud, was that it was unremarkable, and very small. There was (and is) little that was immediately evident or strikingly obvious to have prompted Wellington to have selected it. Only he had! And there was good reason: primarily, Mont-St-Jean's reverse slope; secondly, in front and forward, already tied into the existing terrain, were the stone building strong-point complexes; and finally a restrictively confining battle space, limiting the attacker's manoeuvre options and favouring the defender. Key terrain, obstacles and a narrow choice of enemy avenues of approach were all going to assist Wellington to retain the initiative, to stand up and fight, in the event, to stand-up and fire! Wellington's plan was designed to give his army every chance of standing up and winning.

Commander's intent

'I shall not come with two corps only, but with my whole army, upon this condition, that should the French not attack us on the 18th, we shall attack them on the 19th.'

This dispatch from Blücher received by Wellington in the early hours on the morning of Sunday 18 June was in answer to his letter sent from Quatre Bras requesting the support of two corps of the Prussian Army to support him at Waterloo.

Upon its receipt, and only upon its receipt, did the Duke decide to do battle at Waterloo. Blücher's chief-of-staff, Gneisenau, mistrusted the British, disliked Wellington, and strongly advised Blücher against standing with Wellington at Waterloo. Blücher would not countenance this counsel. His absolute loathing for the French, his desire to atone for defeat at Ligny, and the fact that he personally liked and trusted Wellington, made his decision unambiguous and immediate, besides which Blücher's innate instinct, natural impulse, and integral reasoning were all aligned and he sensed the possibility of victory. As well as his army being 'damnably mauled' by Napoleon, as Wellington said of his defeat at Ligny, Blücher himself had suffered injuries, having been pinned under and trapped by his horse, despite which the 73-year-old warrior was as energized as ever as he drove his somewhat disheartened army forward to keep the promised rendezvous with Wellington. Dispirited by defeat and discouraged by conditions, his 50,000 Prussians were cajoled by him as he coaxed them closer and closer to Waterloo. Because it was he who prevailed upon them, they responded.

Napoleon believed the defeated Blücher would be unable to assist Wellington. His defeat at Ligny would surely not allow this at least for some two or three days. This misapprehension led him to believe he needed only now concern himself with fighting one army, Wellington's, and that he had ample time to do it. Upset as he was at Marshal Ney for not maintaining the tempo of his advance into Belgium towards Brussels, he too sensed victory. It was his intention not simply to defeat Wellington, but to destroy him and his army. A desperation had led Napoleon to force his way through the centre axis via Charleroi up the high road towards Brussels, and so far his direct approach had paid dividends. His intention now was a deadly one. So far, being desperate, direct, and deadly had stood him in good stead. Napoleon's only fear was that Wellington would not offer to do battle. Napoleon eagerly wanted to engage with Wellington, to secure his victory, and to destroy his army.

Wellington had found a low ridge at Mont-St-Jean 20 miles south of Brussels that was favourable for defence. In Wellington's mind putting up a defence meant a delaying of Napoleon. A delayed Napoleon gave time for Blücher and his Prussians to arrive. Time, sufficient or insufficient, was to become the elemental dimension crucial to the success or failure of the battle's outcome. Would Blücher and his Prussians arrive in time, could Wellington defend for sufficient time, and was it possible for Napoleon to destroy Wellington before the Prussians arrived? Only time itself would tell.

THE BATTLE OF
WATERLOO

'A Tradition of Waterloo'

THE BRITISH *army was in position at Waterloo before the French arrived there, and had posted sentries and scouts to watch for the French. At one place there was an outpost of the 14th Hussars, and when the French patrols advanced one of them, an officer on horseback, rode towards the hussars post and challenged any of them to come and fight him man to man. One Irish hussar asked his officer's permission to fight and was granted it, and he rode out and began to slash at the French officer. In the heat of the fight the Frenchman swore in Irish, and the other stopped fighting and asked him was he Irish; he said he was, from such a place, the same townland from which the hussar came. After a few more questions they recognized each other as brothers; the older had gone to France many years before, and the younger joined the British army. They were seen to shake hands. Then they tossed a coin in the air, and both turned and rode back to the British post.* (This tradition was noted from an old man, Thomas Egan, who had heard it many years before from a Waterloo veteran named James Allen, of Derrynasceagh, County Longford) – anonymous writer in *The Irish Sword Vol VIII*, Winter 1967, No.31.

The 'Wild Geese' at Waterloo

Irishmen over the centuries have worn the uniforms of many countries, fought for various diverse causes and been part of armies on separate continents, soldiering under a wide range of different banners, and under none. A history of Irish resistance to outside control of Ireland by the English was to see its victories, but before independence was eventually achieved after many centuries, more than its share of defeats also. This meant that in the lengthy intervening period the major achievements of Irish soldiers were recorded outside of Ireland fighting others' wars – 'for in far foreign fields, from Dunkirk to Belgrade, lie the soldiers and chiefs, of the Irish Brigade'. The beginnings of a tradition of Irish service in Continental European armies can be traced to the mid-17th century, maybe even earlier, with the exodus of 'the Earls' after defeat at the Battle of Kinsale in 1601. Begun in earnest, however, towards the end of the Williamite War of 1689-91, it followed in waves thereafter. A discernible pattern of service abroad with Spain, France, Austria and many other countries far and wide emerged between 1650 and 1800. Generations of Irish soldiers saw service in foreign armies abroad and they were to become known as the 'Wild Geese'. Because this tradition of service was sustained over generations it could involve at any one time, at any one place, in any one army, both native-born and those of Irish descent. Sometimes, tragically, it even involved Irish soldiers in armies facing each other across the same battlefield. It was to France, Ireland's traditional ally, that the greatest number of 'Wild Geese' went. Designated Irish regiments were formed, and some noteworthy involvements followed. The French Revolution was to see this military link severely diminished as the connection had been service to the French Monarchy, which was now deposed. From 1789 on, the Irish regiments in France were disbanded and the long-established connection largely lost. The Bourbon dynasty dethroned, Napoleon was now to the forefront in France. The Napoleonic era, however, was not to be completely devoid of traces of Irish involvement with the French, but was to be in the shape of a newly created 'Legion Irlandaise' (Napoleon's Irish Legion). The Irish Legion was raised in anticipation of a French invasion of Ireland, an expedition that was not to see its original purpose transpire due to the French naval defeat at the Battle of Trafalgar two years later in 1805. The following nine years, up to Napoleon's first abdication in 1814, did see Irish Legion involvement in theatres like Spain but its Irish substance had become severely diluted. Remaining largely in name only, in 1815 the Irish Legion did not have a role in the Waterloo campaign. Interestingly, two French line infantry regiments, the 87eme and 92eme Regiments d'Infanterie de Ligne, post-revolution descendants of the Regiments of Dillon and Walsh, were on the field of Waterloo, but their nature and make-up were entirely French.

Known examples of direct Irish involvement on the side of the French at Waterloo are few. Undoubtedly some were present within the Armée du Nord but few to date have been identified. One such, however, merits mention. Described as 5 foot 7 inches tall (1.7 metres), with blond hair and beard and blue-grey eyes, James MacCarthy was born in Cork in 1784 but had been brought to France at the age of two when his parents decided to settle there. He was thus French raised and certainly bi-lingual, which was probably why he was on demand as a staff officer, serving several generals, such as Morion, Boisserole, and Reille, and was usually requested by name. He was an exceptional soldier by any standard. 'His service record is brilliant. I know of none so distinguished,' wrote William Lawless of James MacCarthy, then a captain of the Irish Regiment's 1st Carabinier Company, when he proposed the promotion of nine captains to lieutenant colonel in early 1813. MacCarthy volunteered as a soldier at 19 in the 24eme Leger at Boulogne (Pas-de-Calais) on 23 December 1803. On his transfer to the Irish Regiment in

December 1809 at the age of 24, MacCarthy was already a chevalier of the Legion of Honour and a veteran of Napoleon's most bitter engagements. He served at the Battle of Waterloo as deputy chief of staff of the 2nd Corps under General Reille. MacCarthy was residing at the time at 23 Rue de Richelieu, Paris 1. He was one of the very few Irish Legion officers to be involved in the battle. In fact, he was one of the very few individuals, and probably the only Irishman, to have served in so many of Napoleons' major battles, including Austerlitz (1805) and Waterloo. Interestingly, at Austerlitz it was the Irish-commanded dragoons that saved the remnants of the Austrian army after Napoleon's greatest victory. James MacCarthy survived the Battle of Waterloo but was unfortunate in his health and suffered from malaria contracted in Zeeland in the Southern Netherlands. He married Alexandrine Rossignol, of a wealthy Parisian legal family. The MacCarthys had four children. He worked for a time with the Depot de la Guerre but appears to have had further health problems preventing him from responding to a recall to the army in 1830. He died five years later. Of the Irish-born officers who served in the Irish Regiment, MacCarthy's short military career was among the most intense.

The Irish lining out among Napoleon's order of battle at Waterloo are very hard to find. It can be a possible conclusion that this is because those were very few of them, whereas, in contrast, the British ranks were crowded with them. The Catholic Relief Act of 1793 especially, but the effects of the French Revolution also, undermined forever Irish recruitment to the French army; instead, the British had found a convenient and ready supply of troops.

Day of the Battle

'Soon after daybreak, I was ordered to take my Company up to the village of Waterloo, to mount guard over the inn occupied by the

Duke of Wellington. As I passed with my men down the front of our line, the soldiers of the different brigades were busily engaged in drying, cleaning, and snapping off their fire-locks which had rusted during the night. Upon reaching the Inn at Waterloo, I drew up in front of the house, and stood at ease for a few minutes; shortly after an ADC came out and told me to return to the field, as the Duke was about to leave his quarters for the army. Almost immediately after my return, and while I was endeavouring to snatch a little rest upon some dry corn sheaves gathered on the way, the first gun was fired from La Belle Alliance.'

If Captain George Cotter, 69th Regiment of Foot, from east Cork had glanced at his timepiece he would have seen it was shortly after half past eleven and made a mental note of it being the time the Battle of Waterloo commenced. The waiting was over. Waiting is the enemy of the soldier. Action, activity, animation of any sort or kind is preferable to biding time, hanging around, remaining in situ, lingering while waiting for orders, be it to retreat, do battle, or whatever the day would bring. In the event, after the appalling torrents of rain during the atrocious overnight weather and a miserable morning to begin with, the wet and shivering soldiers were thankful of a period to dry out, warm up, source some breakfast if they could, and otherwise see to their equipment. For Captain Harry Ross-Lewin, 32nd Foot, from County Clare, and Lieutenants James Colthurst, Jasper Lucas, and Jonathan Jagoe, all from Cork, the early morning of Waterloo was spent trying to dry out their soaked and muddy uniforms after their miserable and largely sleepless night spent out in the open in the relentless rain. For some others, the gin or rum ration dispersed before the battle was the summation of the morning's meal. Corporal Edward Costello, 95th Rifle, from County Laois, remembered that the more inexperienced recruits of his battalion quickly came to rue the fact that they had not thought to take their full share of rations with them when they marched out from Brussels in the early morning on the 16th, two days beforehand. Captain George Cotter continued:

> When the 69th had been formed in column a commissariat wagon came up with a supply of rum for the men; with it came the quarter-master of the Regiment Matthew Stevens, the same who, 18 years before the St Vicent, had broken the stern galley window of the San Nicholas, and led the way for Nelson to the quarter-deck of the Spanish vessel. When the rum had been half served out, a round shot (of French artillery) struck the wagon, and carried off the head of one of the pioneers employed to it. 'Well now,' said the quarter-master, 'it's about time for a peaceable non-combatant like me to gang awa'.

It took time for that shot, along with others, to be fired, because Napoleon's hope of commencing the battle at 9am had been thwarted. Despite brightening horizons, clearing skies and the sun's appearance, the sodden surface soil needed time to dry out. Mud had proved an impediment to progressing his battle plan, and he was forced to postpone its beginning. Instead, he indulged a dramatic display of French imperial might. The splendour of the magnificent spectacle of French martial capacity was to be made obvious to the Anglo-Allied army across the valley and overtly celebrated by the French. Its psychological potential in overawing the Anglo-Allied troops was not lost on Napoleon. Riding on his favourite white horse, Marengo, Napoleon passed his assembled Armée du Nord in review fashion. They in response became filled with enthusiasm, cheered loudly with an eager chorus of 'Vive l'Empereur' as they took up positions for battle. Drums rolled, trumpets sounded, and regimental bands struck up, adding a striking musical dimension to their passionate fervour, ecstasy and emotion. This spontaneous outpouring, an extravagant expression, keenly participated in, was the French allowing themselves an observance of their own self-regard. Their tricolours, military standards, and regimental eagles and pendants, together with the mix of many-coloured uniforms, some complete with striking plumage and shining breastplates, all made for a hugely colourful scene. Altogether, the muddied columns of blue-coated infantry, squadrons of cuirassiers, dragoons, hussars and lancers and artillery, all assembling into battle array with an inherent purposeful intent, were exuding a comfort with their situation. Their flamboyance communicated an ease with their circumstances, – even more, a self-belief in and an assured certainty of a favourable outcome. Napoleon was confident of victory and he was infusing this conviction into his army, all 74,000 of them.

You could not but be impressed by this magnificent high-spirited scene, and many of those of the Anglo-Allied army who witnessed it did feel intimidated, especially those new to battle. For Wellington's veterans of the Peninsular War, those of whom he called his 'Spanish Army', appreciated what they were looking at, maybe even admired it, but were otherwise indifferent. Dazzling displays of soldiers with flags fluttering were all well and good; they knew it was the fighting that mattered and winning the fight that counted. In any event, the vast majority of Wellington's 68,000 army were on the rear slope of Mont-St-Jean and could not see through the hill.

Enthused and excited though the French might be, Wellington was cool and unmoved. Seven years before, in June 1808, Wellington was placed in command of the Peninsular forces. just before he left England, he entertained a colleague to dinner. After the meal he seemed pensive and after a while he was asked what he was thinking about. 'Why, to say the truth,' replied Wellington, 'I'm thinking of the French that I am going to fight. I have not seen them since the campaign in Flanders, when they were capital soldiers, and a dozen years of victory under Bonaparte must have made them better still. They have besides, it seems, a new system of strategy, which has outmanoeuvred and overwhelmed all the armies of Europe. 'Tis enough to make one thoughtful; but no matter, my die is cast, they may overwhelm me but I don't think they will out-manoeuvre me. First, because I am not afraid of them, as everybody else seems to be; and secondly, because if what I hear of their system of manoeuvre be true, I think it a false one as against steady troops. I suspect all the continental armies were more than half beaten before the battle was won. I, at least, will not be frightened beforehand.' Neither was he, soon winning many victories against some of Napoleon's best generals. Applying lessons of organisation regarding supply and transport learned from his campaigning in India, he also showed himself a great and able master of manoeuvre. He was where the action was, moving from position to position, issuing orders, directing matters in person from the front. He employed in defence the 'reverse slope' tactic to very good effect. He improved the system of provisioning, and did not wantingly waste the lives of those serving under him. A disciplinarian, he favoured flogging and abhorred plundering by his troops. They responded favourably to him. 'Old Nosey', he became known to them, and while he maintained a measured distance, a calculated aloofness, they respected him because they had confidence in him. He was proud of them and what they had achieved together. 'I could have done anything with that army,' Wellington used to say in later years, 'it was in such splendid order.' The coming engagement was to be his first direct confrontation with Napoleon and how he wished he had that army with him now. He had a portion of it, the rest newly recruited, untried. Of the allies with him, the British-trained King's German Legion, 6,500 of them, were the ones he trusted; he was unsure of the rest, which is why he referred to his army at Waterloo as 'infamous'. In placing his troops on Mont-St-Jean he endeavoured to ensure that every other one was British, that in as few instances as possible no two (non-British, non-King's German Legion) Allied regiments were side by side. If Wellington had his concerns, so too had Napoleon's marshals who had faced Wellington in the Peninsula, and they attempted to advise Napoleon accordingly. Marshal Soult advocated bringing back the 33,000 men and 98 guns under Marshal Grouchy who were 15 miles to the east, pursuing the Prussians; Marshal Reille cautioned that the British infantry were near impregnable to a frontal assault due to their silent steadfastness and disciplined propensity to produce a constant rapidity of fire, and so suggested manoeuvre. Napoleon poured abrupt scorn on their sound counsel, 'Because you have been beaten by Wellington, you think him a great general.'

Wellington was without Blücher, he was standing alone. Neither did Napoleon imagine Wellington could benefit from the possibility even of the assistance from Blücher and his 50,000 Prussians, believing they would not yet be able to recover from the defeat at Ligny. Even should Blücher decide to assist, Napoleon thought it would take him at least two more days before he could do so. Furthermore, he had set Marshal Grouchy with his 33,000 men and 98 guns on Blücher's heels to prevent any unexpected Prussian appearance on the battlefield from the east. Napoleon's army, as a qualitative collective, were more homogeneous, better experienced, more professional, than Wellington's. In artillery alone, he had more guns, more bigger guns, and better skilled artillery men, in short, a distinct advantage, and it was known 'he could move his guns, with the swiftness of a pistol'. He also considered that Wellington, in deciding to stand, had chosen a poor position to defend, with the forest of Soignes at his back making retreat difficult, if not impossible. Nonetheless, Napoleon wondered a little: would Wellington's defence be better than his attack, could Anglo-Allied endurance beat French élan; was it possible for Wellington to keep intact what he intended to smash? He doubted it. Napoleon was supremely confident of victory. 'There are ninety chances in our favour,' he told his generals. Napoleon's main concern was that during the previous night Wellington might have again slipped away. Napoleon considered it fortunate that Wellington stood, exclaiming delightedly, 'Ah! Now I've got them, those English.' As far as Napoleon was concerned, Wellington stood alone, had positioned himself poorly, and had an inferior army. 'There is no longer time for them to retreat. Wellington has gambled and lost. He has made defeat certain.'

On the other side of the shallow valley the Anglo-Allied army (68,000, of which 28,000 were British) was also taking up its position, having been prevented from doing so previously by the preceding night's thunderstorm, and Wellington was waiting on Blücher's confirmation of support. These matters now settled, Wellington's staff set about organising his position to receive the French assault, and as far as Wellington was concerned, 'the French were going to get the devil of a surprise when they see how I defend a position.' To do so of course, he needed as many troops as possible, in particular British troops and 'enough of them' (hard core, professional, well-trained, experienced and reliable). That Wellington had just 'enough of them' was because many 'of them' had undertaken and endured forced marches in order to arrive at the Waterloo position late on the evening of 17 June, some even in the morning of 18 June itself. The Irish 1st battalion of the 27th (Inniskillings) Regiment of Foot endured a gruelling 51-mile march from the Belgian town of Ghent in a little over two days and two nights, with only two brief halts along the way, arriving at eleven o'clock on the morning of the 18th. Originally held in reserve, a thousand metres to the rear, they were to be ordered forward into the centre of Wellington's line in the middle of the afternoon, thereupon marching into the annals of military history, deploying to display, as a proud Captain Harry Ross-Lewin remarked, 'a fine example of steadiness, discipline and passive courage' during an appalling ordeal. As Lieutenant Edward Drewe of the Inniskillings himself said, the 27th were 'exposed…to all that came' and much French artillery and musket fire did come their way, leading them to suffer enormous losses – 493 casualties out of the 747, a huge tally of dead and wounded, making it seem, as another observer put it, 'the twenty-seventh regiment were literally lying dead in square'. It was a noble record of stubborn defence. Other regiments and brigades had forced-marched for thirty six hours to get there on time. But arrive they did, to play their part in the Duke's defence.

Some 8,000 Irishmen were taking up their positions along Wellington's line. Major General Denis Pack, 9th Brigade, 'scarred with wounds and covered in glory', was to become heavily involved in the battle as he had been at Quatre Bras. His brigade at Waterloo was part of Lieutenant General Sir Thomas Picton's 5th Reserve Division. Picton was to be killed and Pack himself was to be wounded but remained on the field with his command until the close of battle. Also, Major General Sir William Ponsonby was settling his Union Brigade, part of the heavy cavalry, the parent formation of the 6th (Inniskillings) Dragoons, the 'Rollicking Paddies'. During the famous charge of the British heavy cavalry at Waterloo, Major General Ponsonby was to become the most high profile Irish fatality of the campaign. Meanwhile the 18th (King's Irish) Hussars, known among military contemporaries as the 'Drogheda Light Horse' or the 'Drogheda Cossacks', after their regimental colonel, the Earl of Drogheda, were initially stationed on the extreme left of Wellington's line. It was here on the defence's eastern flank that the Prussian troops of Blücher's army would arrive, if they were to arrive. Towards the evening, this Irish light cavalry regiment was to put in a costly charge, but an ultimately successful one. Also on the left in support of Saxe-Weinmar's Dutch Belgian brigade in the Papelotte farm and the houses and farm buildings around it, Wellington placed the 4th and 6th Cavalry Brigades, the 4th commanded by Major General Sir John Vandeleur. They consisted of three regiments of light dragoons or around 1,300 troopers altogether each.

Pack, Ponsonby, Vandeleur, all three above named Irishmen, were highly experienced commanders by 1815, having seen committed service during the Peninsula War and prior to that. General Sir Galbraith Lowry Cole, Dublin-born of an influential County Fermanagh family, had commanded the 4th British Division during the Peninsular War, and was due to command the 6th British Division in Wellington's army. He was, however, in England getting married in mid-June and so missed Napoleon's pre-emptive surprise advance into Belgium. And one other senior subordinate of Wellington at Waterloo was Major General Barnes, known as 'our fire-eating adjutant-general', who appears to have been of Irish extraction.

At the next level down, at battalion and regimental commander level, Lieutenant Colonel John Millet Hammerton, County Tipperary, was commanding the 2nd battalion of the 44th Foot, part of Wellington's centre-left. After he was wounded during the battle, command of the battalion passed to another Irishman, Major George O'Malley from County Mayo. From County Donegal, Lieutenant Colonel Sir Andrew Barnard commanded the green-jacketed rifleman of the 1st Battalion who took up a central position in the line. As sharp-shooting skirmishers, or light infantry, had an additional function to provide a forward screen and to counter their French counterparts. Major Arthur Rowley Heyland of County Derry was killed in action at the close of battle leading the 1st Battalion of the 40th Foot; one of those who contributed to lead their steadfast defence of an exposed position was Captain Conyngham Ellis from Abbeyfeale, County Limerick. So many officers of the 27th (Inniskillings) Regiment of Foot had been killed or wounded by the close of the battle, 16 out of 19, that much of the unit was eventually commanded by its non-commissioned officers instead.

The 13th Light Dragoons could boast of an Irish commander also, Lieutenant Colonel Patrick Doherty, and of the four other Irish officers of the unit, two were his sons, both of whom were wounded. Lieutenant Colonel Henry Murray commanded the 18th Hussars, part of Vivian's Cavalry Brigade, and was on the furthermost left portion. In addition, many aides-de-camp to British brigade or divisional commanders, staff and other support appointments were populated by Irish officers. One such was Major Dawson Kelly, 73rd Foot, and towards the close of battle a sergeant of his regiment came and told him that all the officers of the 73rd were killed or wounded. Although serving on the staff as deputy-assistant quartermaster, he immediately went and took over command.

Prominent at Waterloo, the Irish participation was extensive and as the battles outcome hung in the balance this marked Irish involvement continued to remain significant. For now, the day of battle had dawned and the Irish were there in numbers to contribute towards victory.

Wellington, fearing Napoleon manoeuvring on his west flank, had taken precautions but had also designed his defence to be attacked head-on, and Napoleon's blatantly brutal battle plan was going to oblige him. Napoleon, 'the thunderbolt of war', was about

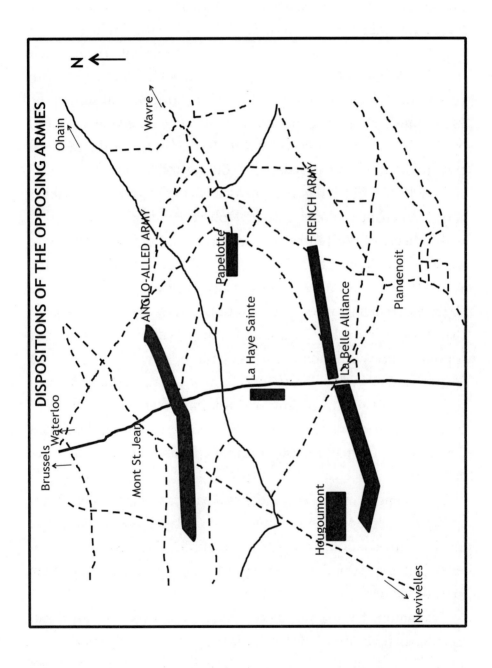

DISPOSITIONS OF THE OPPOSING ARMIES

to bring a new meaning to ferocity; his much anticipated, eagerly awaited 'bloody day' was about to begin.

'A Bloody Day' begins

Strong-points, three of them, naturally occurring and embedded, left, centre, and right, along Wellington's defensive line, granted it additional strength. The château at Hougoumont, the farmhouse at La Haye Sainte, and the farm hamlet at Papelotte, these three structures with their associated out-buildings secured Wellington's defence more steadfastly in place. As blocking positions in good defensive terrain, they firmly fixed the overall defensive line. The immediate purpose of Wellington's defence was to counter Napoleon's attack, to resist his offensive action, to disrupt and frustrate his intention. Wellington needed to deliberately hold Napoleon in check, to gain time until the arrival of the Prussians onto the battlefield, and then together defeat the French.

Key to retaining his defensive initiative was the control of critical terrain. These three strong points were central to this physical posture, as they granted a distinct disruptive advantage in countering the French momentum. They could spoil the synchronization of massed French infantry attackers, narrowing the point of attack of their efforts, canalising them, preventing them concentrating their combat power against any and every part of Wellington's defence of their choosing and forcing them to go where Wellington wanted them to go. Fundamental to defence is the use of combined fire powers, both infantry and artillery, separately or together, but especially in combination with obstacles. This integrated Wellington's fire-planning with his obstacle-planning to the best possible effect allowed by the terrain. Artillery also provided close support in particularly vulnerable areas, those considered to be ones with a higher likelihood of attempted penetration by the enemy – in this case on the right of Wellington's defensive line. By concentrating his infantry, he could mass their fire power at important places at crucial times. By being able to influence the enemy's approach to his defensive line, by being able to corral them to confirmed corridors between the strong points, the more effective his fire power could be on the French assaults.

As part of his fire-planning Wellington gave an order confining his artillerymen to firing only on advancing French troops. They were strictly forbidden to engage in counter-battery or artillery duelling with the French. He wanted to concentrate his fire power on whatever advanced into his defensive line and did not wish to lose individual cannon guns and batteries in unnecessary, uncoordinated 'contacts'. They were also instructed by him that if their positions were overrun during enemy advances, as they were likely to be, placed as they were out in front of the ridge line on the forward slope of the hill, they were to leave their guns and seek shelter inside the infantry squares formed by the respective regiments they were in direct support to, and to re-emerge, taking back up positions along their gun lines to fire on the retreating French, once they had been repelled.

Wellington had just over 150 (157) cannon guns at Waterloo, Napoleon had just under 250 (246). Wellington's were a combination of nine-pounders and six-pounders, Napoleon had twelve-pounders among his artillery. Different guns, used differently, Napoleon liked to fire his twelve-pounders massed together, concentrated in a Grand Battery, while Wellington had his artillery dispersed along his line, with the greater number on his right. In the given situation, Wellington's artillery was used defensively, Napoleon's offensively. Artillery of the time had an effective range of just in excess of 1,200 yards, but the round shot, a solid iron ball, could bounce on dry ground and roll for distances beyond a mile. Frequently, however, they were fired at shorter ranges, and due to Waterloo's compactness as a battlefield, the French gun line of massed artillery was only 900 yards or so away from the ridge of Mont-St-Jean. Fired at much shorter ranges, 100 yards and less, 50 metres mostly, was canister, sometime called case shot or grapeshot. This projectile was a cylindrical tin case filled with small iron balls that scattered immediately on leaving the cannon's muzzle in a short-range, shot-gun like effect, hugely detrimental to closely packed infantry columns. A third type was shell, a hollow iron sphere filled with explosive, detonated by means of a fuse cut to length, which was lit before it was fired. The fuses, however, were frequently inaccurate and otherwise often prone to blowing out. Round shot, canister, and shell were employed by most of the European armies of the Napoleonic era, but the British had a secret projectile called shrapnel. Named after its inventor, it was a mixture of canister and shell, an iron sphere filled with small balls and pre-set fuses that allowed air-bursts to target enemy in cover behind hills. Artillery pieces themselves were of two types, both fixed line-of-sight, fired directly at the enemy by cannons guns or lobbed in an arched trajectory by howitzers which had a shorter barrel. A British battery normally had five cannon guns and one howitzer, while the French equivalent had five cannon guns and two howitzers.

To inflict death, disorientation, and disorganisation was the aim of artillery, and in order to cause further disarray skirmishers (*terailleurs*, or *voltigeurs* being the French names) were typically sent forward to cause further disruption to the defensive line in advance of the arrival of the more formally organised attacking infantry columns. These columns, having marched forward to within 100 yards or so, would form into line and begin to pour fire into the enemy who, if their ranks had not already wavered and broken, would be assaulted by them with bayonets, and the position overrun. As the columns advanced they would be accompanied by cavalry and horse artillery support, the latter periodically deploying quickly to give artillery support fires. These would really come into full effect against massed infantry formed in squares to defend against the approaching cavalry – that is, if they had not already began to be routed by a carefully timed cavalry attack on the vulnerable line, pressed home by the infantry's bayonet charge. Attack was all about fire power, momentum and timing, more precisely its accurate co-ordination at critical moments. Effectively executed, it is near to impossible to defend against. Even though defenders see the attack approach and know what to expect, it can be difficult to counter. Napoleon had repeated success after success since 1808 because of how he chose to attack. However, if a defender could upset the sequencing of this execution of the attack, particularly with the defending infantry remaining steady and disciplined and delivering a consistency in their fire power, allowing their artillery to use the devastatingly effective canister on the advancing cavalry, then they could send into this disorganisation cavalry of their own and thus catch the attacking infantry, still in closed ranks. This type of a counter-charge could change the outcome. It was all to play for in the midst of the melee, where control, courage, and clear-headedness counted. He who applied his plan best, won. A central part to Wellington's defensive plan was the incorporation into his defensive line of the three well-protected strong points. The primary requirement of any strong-point is that it should not be easily overrun. It was highly likely any one or all three strong points would be bypassed, maybe even surrounded for durations during the coming battle, but they must not be overtaken and occupied by the French. Their purpose was to deny access to designated avenues of approach, to corral the French assault into corridors, to hold out in their self-protected spheres for a duration, and then provide a pivot for a counter-attacking manoeuvre.

Wellington, in setting out his defensive plan, had to accept risk in some area in order to concentrate for likely decisive action elsewhere. One such area of risk, more so than any other, was on Wellington's right flank. The ridge of Mont-St-Jean was not straight but rather slightly curved, the right and left flanks slightly further forward than the centre, and 400 yards forward of the right flank was the château complex of Hougoumont. The château had a chapel attached, with barns, storerooms, animal sheds, and the gardeners' and farmers' houses situated around a courtyard. A substantial outer brick wall encircled the entire enclosure, a sturdy stockade highly suited to being defended. Beyond the buildings were a kitchen garden, orchard, and a not insignificant wood. It was essential to defend this since, if left unoccupied, Wellington's entire right flank could be compromised, exposing the exploitation by the French of a shallow valley beyond, leading around rearwards of Mont-St-Jean. Wellington allocated artillery fire support to cover this danger and placed the highly reliable Coldstream Guards as the lead defensive unit to prevent putting his right flank in peril. Hougoumont was in fact nearer to the French line than it was to the Anglo-Allied line, a situation not everyone would feel happy to be in. Neither had it escaped Napoleon's notice!

Napoleon, however, in the first instance, sought to deceive. His primary effort was to effect a false perception, a ruse to make Wellington believe that an attack on Hougoumont, on Wellington's right flank, was his main effort, and so draw his reserves from the centre. This expected, or at least hoped-for reaction could then be leveraged to Napoleon's advantage by a direct classical assault of concentrated massed infantry on Wellington's centre-left. Napoleon's simple plan was to pretend, to pulverise, and to penetrate – a feint on Wellington's right, a massive artillery barrage on his centre-left, and a massed infantry shock attack as a follow-

Closing the Gate at Hougoumont by Robert Gibb, National Museums Scotland.

up. This was to be a battle of annihilation, not over-elaboration. Napoleon had decided that his battle plan was neither to be one of delicately manipulated manoeuvre nor one of complicated multi-phased intricacies; instead, it was going to rely on heavy artillery and brutal bludgeoning by massed infantry attack. He intended to apply direct offensive force to buckle and crumple the Anglo-Allied line. He was going to use overwhelming power to achieve rapid dominance to destroy Wellington's army. Napoleon's plan was to pulverise with cannon to perforate Wellington's line, then penetrate with infantry to pierce it, next to exploit with cavalry to expand the advantage gained and drive home the victory. But first the feint on Hougoumont.

If the attack on Hougoumont succeeded in its own right, well and good, and it was no less serious an assault for either the attackers or the defenders for it being a diversionary one. It was to become a day-long battle within the battle, concurrent with the various developing phases of the day's fighting.

Among Hougoumont's lead defending garrison of the 2nd Battalion of the 2nd (Coldstream) Regiment of Foot Guards were two brothers, James and Joseph Graham, from Clones, County Monaghan, and Ensign James Harvey from County Wexford, a cousin and future brother-in-law of Lieutenant William Harvey (RA). At 11.35am they were to witness a sudden sharp disorder occurring. French artillery began indiscriminate fire from along a gun line formed forward of D'Erlon's corps position. Anticipated as it was, for this is how battles began, it nonetheless caused all three of them to physically shudder and feel a nervous excitement, alert as they were to the feared effects of artillery fire, its violent impact, the collision of iron spheres propelled against human frames, and the deathly destruction of life. The Battle of Waterloo had begun.

Upwards of five thousand troops in seven battalions of French light infantry attacked through the woods surrounding the château of Hougoumont. The diversionary attack was the responsibility of Prince Jerome, Napoleon's brother. General Bauduin led the first wave which, though it pressed hard, did not meet with success, he himself being killed, the first general to die on the battlefield. British howitzers poured shellfire on them from a distance while the defenders poured musket fire on them through loopholes made in the stout stone walls and from the roofs, windows, doorways, and platforms erected as firing steps to fire over the walls. The second French wave, consisting of 3,500 troops, plus the remnants from the previous assault, this time under General Soye, some six battalions, took a different point of attack on the western side of the château. The fighting, no less severe, was more successful for the French, a number of them managing to break through the North Gate, used as an on-going access to allow resupply of ammunition and casualty evacuation. Using an axe, a Lieutenant Legro, 'l'Enforceur' (the Enforcer), broke through the wooden gate and the French began to pour into the courtyard to exploit their forced entry. It was a critical moment. Wellington's right flank was in jeopardy, and the now vulnerable defenders needed to swiftly block this breach before they were overrun. With ten men in all, including three Irish, the garrison commander Lieutenant Colonel MacDonnell moved quickly and bravely to attempt to arrest the situation. With great perseverance, they fought their way through the incoming French, managing to reach the gate and with great strength push it closed in a fierce tussle. With the gate once again shut after much heaving, pushing, and shoving, the guardsmen quickly piled up everything to hand as a barricade, thus preventing the French further reinforcing those who had gained entry. Those French trapped within had then to be dealt with; all were killed with the exception of a young drummer-boy.

During the continuing fighting at Hougoumont, Corporal James Graham was to become further noticed when he saved the life of a Captain Wynham by shooting dead his would-be killer who had his musket raised and was taking careful aim at the officer. Later still, in mid-afternoon during severe fighting, fire broke out in one of the farm buildings being used as a temporary shelter for wounded soldiers, one of whom was Corporal James Graham's brother, Joseph. In the ranks along the garden wall in the thick of the fighting he requested permission from Lieutenant Colonel MacDonnell to be allowed rescue his brother. Permission granted, he successful pulled his brother clear of the burning building and quickly returned to take up the defence. With part of the farm on fire, a dangerous situation presented and Wellington sent a message, written in pencil on donkey skin which on its receipt could then be rubbed out by the recipient so that a reply could be written. It survives still in the British museum and remains legible:

> I see that the fire has communicated from the hay stack to the roof of the château. You must however keep your men in those parts to which the fire does not reach. Take care that no men are lost by the falling in of the roof or floors. After they will have fallen in occupy the ruined walls inside the garden; particularly if it should be possible for the enemy to fire through the Timbers in the inside of the house.

The bravery displayed by Corporal James Graham earned him a unique distinction, his noteworthy actions being entered into his service record, now held at the Public Records Office, with the words: 'The most valorous NCO at the battle of Waterloo selected by the Duke of Wellington'. The Rector of Framlingham in Suffolk, Reverend John Norcross, in early August 1815 wrote a letter to the Duke of Wellington while the Anglo-Allied army was at Paris, expressing his wish to confer a pension of ten pounds a year for life on some Waterloo soldier to be named by His Grace The duke requested a man be chosen from the 2nd Brigade of Guards which had so highly distinguished itself in the defence of Hougoumont. Corporal (later Sergeant) James Graham of the Light Company of the Coldstream Guards was selected, having been nominated by Lieutenant Colonel MacDonnell. Unfortunately, the annuity was paid to Sergeant Graham for only two years, ending because the donor fell into bankruptcy.

Somewhat out of the ordinary for a British soldier of the Napoleonic era, Sergeant Graham's portrait was painted, and it is held, but not on display, at the National Gallery of Ireland in Dublin. Wellington after the battle said, 'The success of the Battle of Waterloo turned on the closing of the gates [at Hougoumont]... no troops could have held Hougoumont but the British, and only the best of them.' It may have been that this statement was uppermost in the minds of the newspaper obituary writers who, when Sergeant James Graham died as an in-patient of the Royal Hospital Kilmainham in Dublin, paid fulsome tribute to the soldier, one writer describing him as 'the bravest of the brave at Waterloo', a tribute paid to very few ordinary soldiers of the period.

Today Corporal Graham is still commemorated in the Coldstream Guards. Each December the regiment marks its historic involvement at Waterloo, in particular the successful closure of the North Gate, with a lively celebration involving senior NCOs taking custody of a brick supposedly from Hougoumont and challenging other ranks to 'capture' the trophy back. This 'hanging the brick', a colourful ceremony, is a contemporary connection to the courage of Sergeant Graham. In 2004 a new accommodation block for soldiers of the Coldstream Guards at Aldershot in Hampshire was named after the Irishman. On his death Sergeant Graham was buried in the soldiers' cemetery of the Royal Hospital Kilmainham.

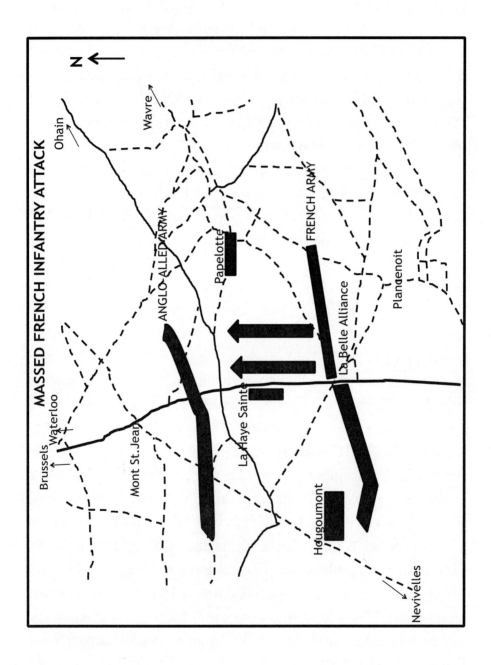

MASSED FRENCH INFANTRY ATTACK

The fight for the control of the château complex at Hougoumont became a battle within a battle and was to continue all day. Some 2,000 Anglo-Allied troops, with the Coldstream Guards in the lead, stood firm defending this strong-point against repeated French assaults. The French persisted in their attempts to capture Hougoumont and committed far more troops than they should have. Instead of it being the diversionary attack it was supposed to be, sucking in Anglo-Allied reserve troops from the centre, the French allowed themselves to become somewhat diverted in their focus, feeding in troops that would have been better employed in bolstering up their main effort in the centre.

One Irish hero had emerged from the repeated attacks on the Hougoumont strong-point. There would be more.

D'Erlon's Attack – the Mud, the Blood, and the Madness

Raw, raucous and reverberating, an alarming audible shock assaulted all the Anglo-Allies' senses. A pervasive percussive pandemonium pierced each defender. The ferocity of the fire-power was felt as much as heard; the staccato sharpness of sound was shrill and it screeched at the nerve-endings throughout the entire body. It was the commotion caused by a massed French cannonade; Napoleon's Grand Battery had opened up. Lieutenant Colonel Henry Murray, 18th Hussars, described the noise as 'deafening'. It was an uproar, a loud and continuous commotion; the 'boom' of the discharge of artillery followed by the explosion of shell was a sensation that was experienced more than heard. Napoleon was putting concentrated heavy artillery fire where he next intended putting his massed infantry.

Napoleon was employing his 'beautiful daughters' (*les belles filles de l' Empereur*), his twelve-pounder cannon guns massed with other artillery drawn up within 900 yards of Mont-St-Jean, hauled into place on a rise slightly east of La Belle Alliance to smash a single point on Wellington's line, to weaken the Anglo-Allied defenders along it by killing as many as possible and demoralising the rest. 'It is with artillery that one makes war,' Napoleon, himself an artillery officer, had stated. Ripple fire was first employed, all 80 or so guns engaging sequentially, 'firing for effect', having first observed the initial fall of shot and making corrections to the target areas. The guns' crews worked with mechanical exactness, repositioning and relaying each gun after its violent recoil, as its deadly discharge, twelve, nine and six -pound iron balls, arched across the valley seeking to smash soldiers' mortal bodies into souls, and otherwise dispirit the rest. It was all part of Napoleon's plan to seriously lessen the Anglo-Allied defenders' physical and psychological will to win. He was intent on employing the shock effect of his massed artillery, followed immediately by the awe of a direct massive infantry assault. His main attack had begun.

A straight-forward plan, well resourced, well led, and well executed, has every chance of success. The scale at which Napoleon had planned his, he thought it invincible. Powerful pre-attack artillery fires and on-going support, a strong screen of skirmishers out in front, an unprecedented and an unstoppable massed infantry attack supported by cavalry must provide an early and decisive blow. He was going to force Wellington's centre-left with a ruthlessly delivered violence. Napoleon, confident in his decision, gave orders for its implementation.

As the thunderous noise and tremendous intensity of the torrid artillery barrage continued, Marshal Ney ordered the light infantry, the skirmishers and sharp-shooters, forward to harass the defensive line in advance of the arrival of the closely packed, formally organised infantry columns. They were sent to seek out and kill especially Anglo-Allied officers, NCOs, and members of colour parties, or any other 'opportunity targets' presenting themselves, but more essentially to inflict casualties along the line of defenders, precisely to goad the front ranks of the defensive line into firing off their first and best-loaded fuselage, giving their own near-advancing massed columns a better chance with a carefully timed final assault. British light infantry had been trained and formed to act against them. One company of each infantry battalion was designated. At Waterloo almost three full 95th Infantry Regiment of Foot (Rifles) battalions were present, the 1st Battalion led by Lieutenant Colonel Sir Andrew Barnard from Fahan, County Donegal, who was to be wounded at Waterloo. Of all the officers present on the battlefield that day, the background of Lieutenant John Molloy must surely be one of the more interesting and curious. Apparently raised in England by an Irish family, he was one of the very few men, it has been claimed, to have been at the battles of both Trafalgar and Waterloo, two of the most significant confrontations of the Napoleonic wars. It was alleged that he was the illegitimate grandson of the then reigning King of England, King George III (and son of Prince Fredrick and the Countess of Tyrconnell, Susanna Hussey). Also with the 1st Battalion '95th Rifles' was Private Edward Costello from Mountmellick, County Laois, Robert J.N. Kellett, Lota House, Lotabeg, Tivoli, Cork, and Captain Nicholas Coldthurst Travers, Dripsey Castle, who came from a family that had incredible military careers. They, as it happened, were connected to the Stawells of Kilbrittain Castle and the Hodders. A cousin, Captain Boyle Travers descended from Boyle Travers of Bandon, was also in the 95th Rifles.

All these men along with their comrades were deployed in and near the sand-pit opposite the farmhouse of La Haye Sainte, the strong-point at the centre of Wellington's line. They were among the few who had sight of the advancing French columns, an intimidating, discouraging, and daunting spectacle. Deployed on the forward slope in a counter-skirmishing role they had a good view of the huge mass of marching men coming at them. With its sheer momentum and the appearance of overwhelming power, it looked invincible. The 95th were armed with the Baker Rifle, different from the 'Brown Bess'. The 'Baker' had a shorter but rifled barrel, grooved to make the ball spin in flight and so was more accurate, and, had a greater range, but it was slower to load. Not only could the 95th see the French advance; like all those behind the hill's crest they could hear it also. Threatening, menacing, sinister, the ominous drub of the French drummers beating the once heard, never to be forgotten, rhythm of the *pas de charge* indicating that trouble was imminent. Rum dum, Rum dum, Rummadum, dummadum, dum, dum, then a pause, followed by shouts of 'Vive l'Empereur'; it was as if the devil was rising up from out of the ground. Danger was on its way and it would not be long in arriving, and it was the kind of danger that wanted to kill you.

Napoleon was staking everything on a frontal shock attack, employing the unimaginative tactics of the battering ram. Four great columns of soldiers, 18,000 French infantrymen in all with lancer and cuirassiers cavalry support on their flanks, went forward, the massive assault in motion. The momentum initiated, each succeeding forward step added to the impending sense of inevitability. The course was set for the impact of motion crashing against obstinacy, tenacious attack set against wilful defence.

The design and sequencing of each component part of the attack, the arrangement for the onslaught in a masterful choreography of all the moving parts, Napoleon left to his generals. He had empowered them in what today would be termed 'mission command', the freedom of action to accomplish his plan and concept through aggressively and independently decentralised execution. Experienced as they were in the ways of Wellington from the war in the Iberian Peninsula, they were familiar with and so correctly wary of his defence, cautious of his deployment, and attentive as to how he had positioned himself for action, so they adapted the size and shape of their attacking formation. Four massive columns advanced together but separately, in echelon, each column detached from one another but connected in overall in a particular order, arranged so they would hit Wellington's line sequentially. Ordinarily, columns advanced with a narrow frontage and extended rearwards over a distance behind. Now, however, depth was traded for width, the better to bring more guns to bear. When advancing, each column appeared as if its broadside was foremost, marching as if sideways was to the front, numerically presenting a battalion frontage with fewer lines behind. However arranged, the French infantrymen within were ebullient, full of high spirits, encouraged by their officers, enthused by their bands and drummers, reassured by the constant rumble of their great guns in support and cavalry on their flanks. The purpose of column formation was to get as much of the mass of men together to within firing range of the Anglo-Allied line. If all went well, and it had every prospect of doing so, they may even smash the defence without having to deploy into line to fire on them. The disciplined, aggressive cohesion of the massive columns looked terrifyingly unconquerable, creating an overwhelming sense of jeopardy that in past battles had caused defenders to flee even before the assault's culmination. Now with the use of weight of numbers on a grand scale coming at his defensive line, it was what Wellington had spoken of seven years beforehand, prior to his departure to the Peninsular War in 1808, only now unimaginably magnified. It was as if he had waited all his life for this moment and here it was coming head-on at him. Outmanoeuvred he was not going to be. Napoleon had chosen to go directly for him, but would he be overwhelmed? Would his quick-firing infantry stand firm? He was sure that the British and King's German Legion would, but would that be enough?

Seemingly unassailable, the French presented an intimidating steamrolling formation with strength of numbers that must surely flatten any resistance to it beneath its huge mass. This bludgeoning tactic was battle-proven and today its escalation ought to extend its effect. The cacophony of the continuous cannonade fire spewing lethal round shot, shell, and thick smoke across the valley onto Mont-St-Jean, suddenly subsided as the French columns re-emerged into view from the valley floor. It was now the turn of the Allied artillery to open fire, only there were far fewer guns on the centre-left to do so. The mud on the up-hill slope with the head-high rye made the French infantry progress more ponderous, however, slowing their rate of advance and allowing more time for the allied guns to play on them. The left-hand leading French column nearest to La Haye Sainte tied up the attentions of the Anglo-Allied centre, while the main body of the attack, the other three columns, swept past and up the muddy slope. It would soon be time for the columns to deploy into line but for now it was all about advance. Making headway become more contested, however, as the tempting target of the large-scale, densely-packed columns of French infantry was irresistible to the 24 guns of the Anglo-Allied artillery along the centre-left line, and their fire tore holes in the advancing French column formations. Where gaps appeared in the columns the spaces were filled from within, being 'closed-up' immediately. The defenders' cannons roared but still the French came on. It was uninterrupted cannon fire against unceasing momentum, the monstrous mass of French infantry stepping ever closer. It was time now for canister, and the gun crews 'double-loaded', putting both cannon ball and canister into the gun muzzles and firing both at once. Devastation and death followed, the cost in French dead and wounded huge, but still the super-sized French columns advanced. It seemed the momentum of the French attack must carry them over the ridge, sweeping all before them. Bylandt's Dutch-Belgian brigade broke and fled, bolting rearwards, a dangerous gap opening up in the Anglo-Allied line. Victory for the French appeared within touching distance. From Napoleon's viewing point at La Belle Alliance a breakthrough by undeployed column seemed in sight. Napoleon's hammer-blow was set to strike home. French infantry were cascading forward with certainty, about to crash through the Anglo-Allied line. Only there was no line, but there was a hedge. This was not a formidable impediment but it was an obstacle that had to be negotiated. That no Anglo-Allied line was apparent was an illusion; they could not see it, not because it was not there, but because it was lying down a hundred or so yards to the rear, sheltering from the massive French cannonade. They were Kempt's Eighth Brigade consisting of the 32nd, 79th and 28th regiments of foot, and further left to the east, Pack's Ninth Brigade consisting of the 1st, 42nd, 92nd, and 44th regiments of foot. The 95th Rifles had re-taken up position also. The division commander Picton now ordered Kempt and Pack to 'arrest the torrent'.

Picton's 'Scotish' Infantry stood up, moving forward to counter the penetration of the Anglo-Allied line, just as the French began an awkward and unwieldy movement to negotiate the hedge. The timing was opportune for the defenders, who moved forward to within 40 yards of the French and on order poured deadly fire into them. The 92nd Gordon Highlanders had been stationed in Ireland and sailed from Cobh on the 1 May 1815, arriving at Ostend on the 7th, two days later going to Ghent and remaining there until the 28th, moving next to Brussels where they were billeted throughout the city until having to move to arrest Napoleon's advance. Among them was Captain Robert Hobbs from Bornaboy, County Offaly, whose wife Margaret (Hackett) was to become the last surviving widow of an officer who had fought at Waterloo. With the 42nd 'Black Watch' Royal Highlanders was Private James Gosnell from Durrus, County Cork, a former shoemaker who had previously joined the South Cork Militia. He was to be wounded in his right leg by a lance at Waterloo but survived. Also present among their ranks was a former tailor's apprentice from Kilkenny, Private David Carroll.

The French momentum became suddenly and unexpectedly immobilised. They were completely stumped by the discharge of three thousand muskets at forty paces. The surprise threw them into confusion. Seizing the moment, Picton ordered a bayonet charge; the French bewilderment gave way to chaos, and they fled.

There was, however, fight left in some. The 'colour' carrier of the of the British 32nd Regiment of Foot was suddenly confronted by a French officer. The capture and carrying off of one's battalion colours was an enormous dishonour and an ignominious humiliation to those who relinquished it, and so in battle its defence could require fanatical gallantry. Lieutenant Robert Tresilion Belcher, 32nd Foot, from Bandon County Cork, had taken the colours from the ensign originally carrying them after he became wounded during the attack. In the next moment it was seized by a French officer whose horse had just been shot under him. A struggle ensued between him and Lieutenant Belcher, and while the Frenchman was attempting to draw his sword the covering colour sergeant gave him a thrust in the chest with his halberd pike (spear-headed staff) and the right-hand man of the sub-division shot him. Lieutenant Belcher received honourable mention by the Duke of Wellington in his reports on the incident.

The two most junior officers of a battalion, each escorted by the two most senior sergeants between them, had the most dangerous of the tasks. They formed the battalion's colour party and carried the battalion's two colours into battle (a practice which ceased in 1881). The capture of a colour was considered a conspicuous conquest. The regimental colours were hugely regarded, consecrated even, and were saluted by all ranks. The regiment was an administrative entity, each having two battalions, one at home and one abroad. Hence the term regiment was interchangeable with battalion. A regiment's colours were a tangible visible emblem in the form of a flag. In the case of those carried by the Irish at Waterloo, they were double-sided silk, six-foot square, carried on a ten-foot pole. The colours represented the regiment's integrity and immortal inner nature; it exemplified the existence of the battalion's permanent primacy above all those who served in it, in turn delivering a source of inspiration, self-respect, worth and esteem. It gave meaning to men in the midst of the madness of mindless battle. Originally devised as a marker, it was a standard around which separated soldiers could rally, and so served to preserve the unity and cohesion of a unit in the heat of the battle. In moments of difficulty and danger it was looked for, and so became looked upon as special. It mattered, because it had a purposeful meaning to the soldiers who fought side by side under it. The danger of carrying the colours were emphasised in another part of the battlefield that day when Ensign William Nettles, 52nd Foot (Light Infantry), one of five sons of Captain Robert Nettles of Nettleville, County Cork, was killed while carrying the King's colours, which were afterwards found under his body. Ensign Peter Cooke, 44th Foot, of Stoutbridge, County Tipperary, had suffered a similar fate two days previously when carrying the King's colours at Quatre Bras.

The other two large French columns now hit the Anglo-Allied centre-left line and there was fighting all along it. Trying to deploy into line, the French columns found the defensive line overlapped them, firing vigorously into their front and flanks and preventing them deploying into line, but they stood their ground and continued to engage. The situation required a battle-defining moment. The Anglo-Allied line was still in peril. Lead musket balls were flying furiously in either direction between attackers and defenders at intimate distances of 50 yards and less. Smoke bellowed from volley fires, the putrid smell of black powder evident everywhere, and the noise of gunfire, the screams of the dying, the shouted orders of officers and NCOs, all filled the crucial moments. With the battle in the balance, its outcome delicately poised, Wellington hurled his horses and 'sabres' (troopers), his heavy cavalry, forward into the fray to support his infantry. The two cavalry brigades of the 'Household' and 'Union' heavy cavalry, Lord Uxbridge's and Sir William Ponsonby's from Cork, drew their sabres from their sheaths, pressed their heels into the sides of their mounts, and charged forward in a tumultuous wave utilising the full momentum of 2,000 horses and riders. With drawn sabres slashing and cutting, they annihilated the now stunned and stalled French infantry and cavalry. This formidable full-on charge of the British heavy cavalry included the involvement of Irish horsemen of the 6th Dragons (Inniskillings), the 'Rollicking Paddies'. Their intervention, along with the rest of the brigade was timely and effective as their mounts crashed into and trampled over the hapless French infantry. Observing the melee, Irish officer Major George de Lacey Evans, aide-de-comp to Sir William Ponsonby, described how 'the enemy fled as a flock of sheep across the valley – quite at the mercy of the dragoons'. This incident of significance involved an Irish officer becoming noted for his gallantry. Captain Edward Kelly, an officer of the 1st Life Guards from Portarlington, County Laois, having distinguished himself previously at Quatre Bras, found himself now, two days later, to the fore of his regiment as they attacked. On the occasion he was responsible for singling out and unhorsing a French colonel. Dismounting in the middle of the action, Kelly removed the Frenchman's epaulettes as a souvenir of his exploit. 'I got his horse also – a most noble one,' he wrote to his wife after the battle, 'but being attacked by a number of French at the same time, I was obliged to let him go.' In the same letter, he used a uniquely Irish phraseology to illustrate the ferocity of the hand-to-hand fighting at Waterloo: 'Donnybrook Fair was nothing to the fight we had here…there was a great number of wigs on the green.' Kelly's bravery led him to becoming relatively famous within the British army, earning the nickname 'Waterloo Kelly', and a number of prints and drawings depicting his heroics were published following the campaign. With this encounter ongoing, the 'Inniskillings' charged in line and Sergeant Major Mathew Marshall's squadron dashed into the thickest of the enemy's phalanx, and were cut off from the other troopers of the 6th Dragoons. Marshall, while thrusting his sabre into a cuirassier on his right, had his bridle arm broken by a stroke from an enemy on his left, and had not proceeded much further when he was beset by a number of French cavalry and hurled from his horse by a lance which penetrated his side. While he was falling he received a heavy blow across the body and another which broke his right thigh. He lay unconscious but was then goaded into sensibility by the hoofs of the French horses passing over his mangled body. The ground afterwards becoming somewhat clear he saw a horse without any rider, which he crawled towards and was about to mount when a French trooper cut him down in midst of his hopes, inflicting several wounds on his body. Despite accumulating 19 wounds in all, he survived, and in contrast to his misfortunes the cavalry charge was a marked success. Napoleon's massed infantry attack, one of gigantic proportions, had been stopped by the heroic defiance of the two-deep line of infantry and the superbly timed and beautifully executed charge of the British heavy cavalry. Hundreds even thousands of French causalities and prisoners resulted, and most importantly the momentum was turned, the initiative regained and Wellington's line remain intact. The heavy cavalry were now stimulated by their success and highly exercised with excitement. Their elation found expression by succumbing to the driving force of the intense impulse to 'head for the guns', Napoleon's twelve pounders, his 'beautiful daughters'. Their training and discipline set aside, instead of rallying and keeping themselves in check to preserve their capability for future action, they went unhesitatingly forward. One hundred yards out they stretched their sword arms fully, sabre tips pointed slightly down, ready to engage, and fixed their minds on the fight ahead. Grapeshot and shell exploded around them sending horses violently onto their backs, legs frantically flaying, riders flung uncontrollably into the air then slammed hard onto the ground, horse and human flesh torn by fragmentations of iron splinters, blood spurting from lacerations, mounts and troopers screaming with shock, fear, and pain. No need now to check spacing and correct dressing of alignment in the advance, it was all about forward momentum, Their 'blood was up', the intoxication of the charge at its height, as they slammed into the French gun line. No time now for reloading their twelve pounders, the French bombardiers desperately reached for their muskets, pistols and swords, but all too belatedly. Slashing British sabres severed French heads and hands in swift execution of what they had been taught at sword drill and learned from former battlefields. The cutting and thrusting continued until French lancers, cuirassiers, and dragoons appeared. And with them the dreaded realisation, with their horses 'blown' (worn-out), they had overextended. It was time to rally if they could, retreat if they could, fight their way back if they could. Lieutenant Colonel Joseph Muter, officer commanding 6th

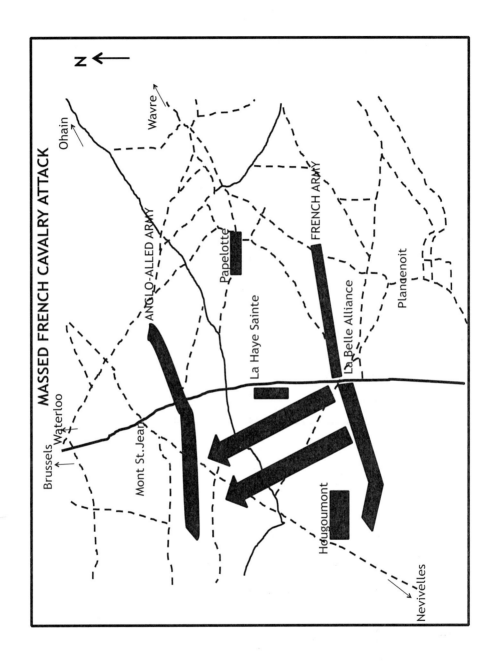

MASSED FRENCH CAVALRY ATTACK

Dragoons, acknowledged afterwards that the Irish horsemen of his regiment, like their peers among the rest of the heavy cavalry, 'went on with so much impetuosity, and suffered severely, both in pursuit and return, from the *peletons*, clouds, or small bodies of French lancers.' The 'Rollicking Paddies' thus ultimately paid a costly price for their charge at Waterloo.

It was during the same charge of the British heavy cavalry at Waterloo that the most high-profile Irish fatality of the campaign occurred. Major General Sir William Ponsonby's Union Brigade, the parent formation of the 6th Dragoons, the Inniskillings, had been at the forefront of the action. While attempting to rally the disordered formation during the latter stages of the charge, he was attacked by French lancers and put to death with a staff officer of his brigade at the wrong end of their long spears. Some accounts have suggested that Sir William was initially taken prisoner but then killed by his captors mindful that approaching British cavalry might affect his rescue. However, more readily accepted is the version that Sir William's getaway was impeded by riding into a muddy ploughed field, enabling his pursuers to catch and kill him. Major George de Lacey Evans was more fortunate and despite a close brush with death himself, his horse receiving a sabre cut across the head, he narrowly escaped death during the frantic withdrawal of the British heavy cavalry. He put forward the suggestion that his superior's officer's unlucky predicament was contributed to by being on a second-rate mount.

> Poor Sir William Ponsonby might perhaps have been spared to his country had he been better mounted. He rode a small bay hack. He had a handsome chestnut charger, which he meant to mount when real business began, but the groom or orderly who had charge of the chestnut was not forthcoming or within call at the moment the General wanted his horse.

The hurried retreat of the remains of the British heavy cavalry after their ill-advised and costly charge required the intervention of Major General Sir John Ormsby Vandeleur, County Laois, and his 4th British Cavalry Brigade, to extract them from their difficulty. Lieutenant John Vandeleur, 12th (Prince of Wales) Regiment of Light Dragoons, Maddenstown, County Kildare, a close relative, also fought at Waterloo. The surviving cavalrymen, about half of whom who charged, scrambled back in complete disorder onto Mont-St-Jean and there reorganised themselves after their wasteful misadventure and causing the unnecessary loss of their comrades. Importantly, however, the Anglo-Allied line remained unbroken, and the French would have to try again. For now an unusual normality descended across the valley, belying the recent bedlam. Matters would settle for a while, but only for a while, as an unexpected whirlwind was about to be let loose.

Cannon Balls and Cold Steel

Seventeen inches of a stabbing blade fixed to a musket could stop a horse advancing at pace dead in its tracks. Singularly, even collectively, troops in line were fatally vulnerable to cavalry assault. A viable defence against a cavalry charge, however, was to form a four-deep hollow square facing outwards. The front two of this four-deep rank formation would kneel with their muskets sloped at an angle of 45 degrees, the tip of their bayonets held at horse-chest height. Psychologically, horses would not advance onto this barricade of bayonets. If those forming the four faces of the square maintained their nerve, this barrier of bayonets could indefinitely deter attacking cavalry. This defence was, of course, complimented by the two rear standing ranks firing for effect over the heads of those kneeling. Heavy cavalry attacking at pace was a formidable and hugely frightening prospect. The natural survival instinct of those within was to break ranks and run for cover. However, by its simple yet clever design, a tightly-packed, four-sided square provided a mutually supporting formation where each men covered the back of his comrades, who in turn, were covering his. This interdependence allied to discipline and leadership were critical to its integrity and survival of those within. A battalion formation of eight companies or more formed a square. Because many battalions had ten companies, two of the squares faces had three, maybe even four companies each, the other two faces being made up of two or one companies each; hence the shape of a square was more often a rectangle. Inside the hollow square, or rectangle, were the regimental colours, the rally-point around which the square was formed, their defence paramount, the horse-mounted officer commanding with other officers on foot providing the necessary command and control element overseeing the letting loose of defensive fuselages. As well as this very necessary fire-control function, officers had to ensure any gaps appearing in the square through causalities were filled immediately to prevent the enemy cavalry probing this vulnerability. The wounded were also pulled into the inner space and, if possible, were assisted before being taken to the rear for medical aid, such as it was. Often this function in the square was performed by the battalion's musicians.

The square's defensive formation could repel wave after wave of horse-born enemy coming at it indefinitely. Cavalry supported by infantry, skirmishers in particular or more onerous again, horse artillery, presented an altogether more formidable challenge, the difficulty being that a square presented a larger, more densely populated target than a two-deep line of infantry. Elements of one's own cavalry and light infantry skirmishers could assist in countering these testing circumstances. Attack and defence were all about the careful synchronisation of all assets to get the best effects in the circumstances prevailing. The tactic was to manipulate the situation to create and seize upon initiative and drive home any advantage . It was also about timing, the difference between victory and defeat often being a few well-executed musket volleys that were better applied than the enemy's. The excellently executed defence by the British 8th, 9th, and Hanoverian 5th Brigades on the ridge's centre-left exemplified this. Wellington's line had undoubtedly buckled severely under the massive weight of attacking French infantry, but furious musket volleys and a ferocious counter-attack backed by the cavalry had held the French assault in check, but only just, and at enormous cost. The first French assault had been defeated. This momentum-changing moment was copper-fastened by the brilliance of the charge of the British heavy cavalry. Their failure to control themselves, however, had exasperated Wellington previously in the Peninsula, and now here again at Waterloo was another dramatic illustration of this self-destructive flaw. The bringing together of the potent combative combination of infantry, cavalry, and artillery at the opportune time could prove pivotal to success, or alternatively disastrous if on the wrong end. At Quarte Bras two days previously, Marshal Ney had moved against the Anglo-Allied squares without infantry or artillery support and so, in the main, lost effectiveness. It was the combined use at the correct moment that was important.

For now, however, as the discharge smoke from the Anglo-Allied defenders' muskets and cannon lay thick across the battlefield, Major General Sir William Ponsonby, brigade commander of the Union Cavalry Brigade, was dead; Major General Denis Pack, brigade commander, 9th Infantry Brigade, was wounded but remained on the field; Major General Sir John Ormsby Vandeleur, 4th Cavalry brigade commander, had covered the bedraggled withdrawal of the remnants of the heavy cavalry brigade, preventing their extermination; Corporal James Graham, Coldstream Guards, had heroically helped close the North Gate at Hougoumont and was continuing the fight; Captain Edward Kelly, 1st Life Guards, had noteworthily unhorsed and captured a French colonel; Lieutenant Robert Tresilin Belcher, 32nd Foot, had successfully defended his regimental colours; Lieutenant Colonel Sir Andrew Barnard had led 'the best skirmishers in the British army', the 1st Battalion 95th Rifles, in a fine example of disciplined and effective use of light infantry; Lieutenant Colonel John Dawson, Earl of Portarlington, officer commanding 23rd Regiment of Light Dragoons, was absent from where his duty required him to be; half of the 6th Dragoons were dead, wounded, captive or missing; Troop Sergeant Major Matthew Marshal was among them, lying out on the valley with no less than 19 wounds in all; Private James Gosnell, 42nd Royal Highlanders, had a French lance stuck into his right leg but along with all other Irish members of the 32nd, 79th, 28th, 1st (42% Irish), 42nd, 92nd, and 44th Regiments of Foot had 'stood firm' in the face of the massive French infantry onslaught; and now the 27th Foot, the Inniskillings, had arrived rested and were moved forward to reinforce the centre of Wellington's line, to fight against whatever next might come. And come it soon would, only no one expected what did come!

About the time of the opening up of the grand battery, Napoleon observed troops moving five miles to the east. For the briefest of moments he thought them to be Marshal Grouchy's 'marching to the sound of the guns' who had come across to support Napoleon from Wavre, but of course almost immediately realised they were the advance guard of the Prussians. Time, and its shortage, had begun to take on a significance, because the Prussians had begun to approach Waterloo. The odds of a French victory, which had earlier been expressed by Napoleon as 'ninety to ten', were now revised downwards by him as 'sixty to forty' – 'This morning we had ninety odds in our favour, we still have sixty against forty.' In his mind, victory was still possible. D'Erlon's unsuccessful massed infantry attack was disappointing but not disastrous, a setback for sure, but not ruinous.

Wellington for his part was relieved, and along with others momentarily believed that the battle itself could well be over. The situation had indeed been critical before the crucial cavalry charge. Steady British infantry and courageous cavalry inflicted much casualty on the French and temporarily broke three divisions of French infantry, completely driving back Napoleon's main attack. Time now to reorganize, regroup, and reinforce. Wellington oversaw much of this himself and once again used the reverse slope as a screen behind which to shield the regrouping of his troops. The crest of Mont-St-Jean appeared largely devoid of activity. Supervising all this physically, he typically was war-gaming Napoleon's possible next move. In the event, his anticipation was to be astonishingly wide of the mark!

Napoleon too was directing, albeit at a distance, the preparations for a new assault on the farmhouse at La Haye Sainte. The Grand Battery had first to be re-aligned, repaired, and added to after the disruption caused to it by the British heavy cavalry attack. It was about this time that the first stirrings of some elements of French cavalry appeared as if they were being made ready for action. The key to the centre of Wellington's line was possession of the farmhouse at La Haye Sainte. In the wake of their failed main infantry attack, the French had, under orders of Napoleon and the command of Marshal Ney, used large numbers of *tirailleurs* to advance in open order east and west up along the main road. Those east of the road were again first met by the 95th Rifles, then the King's German Legion, the actual garrison of the improvised makeshift fortress itself, and finally by Kempt's Brigade advancing in line. Those French attackers west of the road were driven back by artillery fire from British batteries on the height above Hougoumont. It was during this unsuccessful and brief encounter that Napoleon's Grand Battery was being realigned. With the repelling of the attempt to seize the farmhouse, it was nonetheless possible that a further French attack was being arranged. Only there was no sign of French infantry preparations. Instead, puzzlingly, there was further massing of French cavalry. It soon became clear, in so far as anything was clear, that the build-up of strength was of French Cavalry only. The concentration of cavalry without infantry in support was bewildering but what a magnificent sight it made. It was, however, might that mattered and while those few on the ridge of Mont-St-Jean were admiring of the sight they were beginning to become every bit as alarmed.

Approaching four in the afternoon, the French recommenced their cannonade, now able to reach all points along the ridge; the non-arrival of the Prussians onto the battlefield was a worry from Wellington's point of view while its possibility was entirely unwelcome by Napoleon, who had dispatched 12,000 troops to his right flank on the east to guard against any possible intrusion there. Hougoumont was on fire in the west with the fighting drawing in ever increasing numbers of French troops. All of this concurrent activity eroded the strength of Napoleon's infantry to concentrate on the main effort. Like all good commanders he held a reserve, his famed Imperial Guard, and was particular in preserving them until he thought it opportune to commit them into the fray. There was still much fighting to be done and the French capacity to do battle, although dwindling piecemeal, was still to be reckoned with, more especially with Napoleon in command.

The Anglo–Allied army was shaken but not broken. It was the fighter within the soldier that made him continue to function in unfavourable circumstances. On the other hand, the French soldiers had been driven back but were not beaten. It was the resilience and the 'grit' within that gave him the ability to withstand the physical and mental strain. It was the character of their leaders that fortified their resolve. Waterloo was a battlefield where soldiers were slayers, and already considerable carnage had been carried out. There had been much killing done already and the butchery was to continue in what was already becoming a bloodbath of a battle.

Cavalry were designated as 'heavy' and 'light', called dragoons and hussars respectively, depending on the role they were designated to undertake. Heavy cavalry was used primarily for 'set-piece' charges, for the injection of shock and collision in the attack to give momentum and gain the initiative when closing in on infantry. The role of light cavalry was raiding, reconnaissance, and rendering advance posts to protect against surprise and sending out of patrols. The French cavalry more or less mirrored this but had an additional element which the Anglo-Allied army did not, lancers. Nine-foot-long lances gave reach, allowing the spearing of opponents and also the presentation of a fearsome sight, especially terrifying to the inexperienced. In relation to their employment against infantry squares, if even a few of the Anglo-Allied kneeling ranks could be successfully speared, the lances could be dropped and the squadron, pressing in with sabres over the wounded men, could soon complete the destruction of the square.

As the massing of the French cavalry continued, the French intent was becoming more apparent and it at once caused apprehension; most importantly, it demanded a defence. Tactically askew, its asymmetrical nature has been the cause of much historical guesswork by historians since, but Wellington had then to confront what he saw put in front of him, and his answer was artillery, infantry squares, and the getting ready of what was left of his cavalry.

The advance of the French cavalry provided a magnificent but terrifying spectacle, a daunting display of very real might in the form of cold steel of over 5,000 lances and sabres glittering in the long lines. In advance came the cannon balls as the French artillery once again pounded the Anglo-Allied line. Most of the Allied troops could not see the cavalry coming, hidden as they were behind the hill's crest. When the French artillery stopped firing they knew they could not be far away, confirmed for them by the sound of their own artillery on the forward slope opening up, firing as fast as they could load. This too stopped, and over the crest into view came the frantic scrambling run of the 'gunners' seeking the sanctuary of the squares. Then they heard the approaching cavalry 'like the whole of hell coming up out of the ground', the thunderous noise of horse hoofs making the very earth on which they stood vibrate. It caused a strain on their nerves almost beyond endurance. The first line of French horsemen galloped over the horizon and down on them, then more, and behind them more again. The sheer size, speed, and momentum were seriously unsettling for the static troops. But it was a shock too for the French cavalry men to find a chessboard-pattern formation of mutually supporting infantry squares awaiting their arrival. In familiar style they waited until the cavalrymen were within 40 paces and the front kneeling ranks fired, then placed the butts of their muskets on the ground. 'Fire at the horses,' came the shouted order as the standing ranks poured volleys into them. Horses came crashing down and caused those behind to pile up. The storm of musket-fire erupting from the squares killed and wounded horsemen and horses, the curious noise of musket balls hitting the cuirassiers' helmets and breastplates being heard through the din of battle. The lines of French cavalry broke, divided, and veered sideways, sweeping around and past first one, then another, and then throughout all the squares, receiving fire from them as they

Ensign Edward Hodder in later life.

rode by. The bravado of the French cavalrymen waned, hundreds of riders were killed, and foaming, riderless horses were everywhere. The attack receded, the cavalry retreated. The British artillerymen ran back to their guns and 11 batteries got their cannons ready and opened up on the withdrawing French. The squares and gun positions withstood repeated charges executed bravely but foolishly by the French. Lieutenant William Harvey, Lloyd's Brigade Royal Artillery, from Wexford, was one of those who repeatedly reset his battery 'ready for action' on each French retreat. As the battery second-in-command, Captain Samuel Rudyard, described,

> The cuirassier and cavalry might have charged through the battery as often as six or seven times, driving us into the squares, under our guns, wagons, some defending themselves. In general, a squadron or two came up the slope on our immediate front, and at their moving off at the appearance of our cavalry charging, we took advantage to send destruction after them, and when advancing on our fire I have seen four or five men and horses piled upon each other like cards, the men not having been displaced from the saddle, the effect of canister.

Captain Arthur Gore, son of the Honourable Richard Gore, MP for Donegal, was with the 'old three tens' 30th Foot, as was Lieutenant John Rumley from East Cork. An ensign with the regiment gave the following description:

> 'Here comes these fools again,' growled the 30th rank and file as they prepared to pour a destructive fire on the advancing French cuirassiers, which invariably emptied many saddles and sent the remainder from where they came.

When the French cavalry was not charging the Anglo-Allied infantry squares, the French artillery would open fire, and this caused a high casualty rate, so much so that it was preferable to be under attack from the cavalry than under fire from the artillery. The ground was contested and the intensity of the firing throughout the two hours saw charges followed by retreats to be followed by charges again. This sometimes resulted in hand-to-hand fighting between the respective cavalries. The onslaught of cannon balls and cold steel continued, and as the second-in-command of the 69th Foot put it, 'Section after section of the 69th was swept off by the enemy's artillery at Waterloo whilst the French cavalry repeatedly surrounded the devoted Regiment.'

Irish officers serving in the 69th Foot included Captain George Cotter, Cork, Lieutenant Christopher Busteed, Cork, Lieutenant Henry Anderson, Kilkenny, who was slightly wounded at Quatre Bras by a ricocheting bullet and near the close of battle at Waterloo was shot through the left lung, the ball making its exit at the back, breaking the scapula, and Ensign Edward Hodder, Cork, who was to lose his leg.

The Anglo-Allied troops held their ground. The massed cavalry attack, which saw four horses shot out from under Marshal Ney, did not do what the massed French infantry had also not done, and fighting was to end in a kind of curious stalemate, with the cavalry reduced to circling the squares as the infantry held their fire and hurled insults at them instead in a deadly game of 'cat and mouse'; the French would not attempt to penetrate a square where they knew the infantry had loaded muskets and the infantry would not fire on the cavalry, as if they did so the cavalry could attack before they reloaded. This sometimes resulted in both sides simply standing and looking at each other. Deadlock resulting, with both sides suffering and exhausted, no breakthrough was achieved. Marshal Ney, without a horse, walked back across the valley.

No Reinforcements, No Retreat

Time can present opportunity. The opportunity, however, must be quickly grasped or it passes, and a new set of circumstances arises. One such opportunity presented itself for a brief 30 minutes at Waterloo. At 6.30pm La Haye Sainte farmhouse fell, opening the Anglo-Allied centre and putting Wellington into a crisis with Marshal Ney asking Napoleon for reinforcements. For the defenders, these 30 minutes could either see the approach of the French from the front or the Prussians onto the left of the Mont-St-Jean ridge. In the event, both were to happen, but which would happen first?

'Cut up to a skeleton,' is how Sir James Kempt described the state of his division to Wellington, adding, 'My Lord, if I am charged again by the enemy, I am not able to stand.' Wellington answered, 'You must stand while there is a man, and so must I. The Lord send night or Blücher.' While the Prussians were near, they were not nearly near enough. At the same time the Anglo-Allied army was close to the limit of its ability to endure. The situation had gone from standstill to breakpoint. The farmhouse at La Haye Sainte had fallen, and the positioning of French horse artillery beyond it had broken the deadlock and was causing carnage. Napoleon's 'battle of annihilation' had turned into Wellington's 'battle of attrition'. The standing strength of the Anglo-Allied army was severely diminished and they were literally bleeding to death on Mont-St-Jean. The continuous loss of personnel and equipment, the constant wearing down of their reserves and resolve, was bringing them to the point of collapse.

Yet another dogged French attack on the farmhouse of La Haye Sainte had been pressed by the French. Marshal Ney under orders from Napoleon was determined to secure the key to the centre of the battlefield. Although displaying great bravery, he had failed to secure anything all day and was resolute in his efforts to gain the strong-point. The British artillerymen were staggered that the French cavalry during their earlier continued sequence of charges, having repeatedly overrun the guns, did not drag any of them away or render them useless. The British infantrymen in squares, although suffering the effects of the pounding from the Grand Battery, were thankful and mystified, all at once, that the French had not brought up their horse artillery. They had not neglected to do so again and were making great advantage with it. The new attack on the farmhouse had succeeded largely because the King's German Legion defenders, having successfully and ferociously protected the strong-point against almost continual attack all day, ran out of ammunition for their Baker Rifles.

The farmhouse was in French hands and they were exacting considerable advantage from its possession, particularly the occupation of nearby firing points for their horse artillery. Its seizure gave their attack a renewed vigour. They had battered the Anglo-Allied line with massive resources using great weight of numbers in what, however, had been somewhat disjointed efforts, but now they felt they were on the verge of victory. The outcome of the battle was hanging by the thinnest of threads. The final blow must come and would surely tell. The constant wearing away of Anglo-Allied numbers and nerves was taking effect. The day-long fighting had caused great fatigue, exhausting Anglo-Allied reserves of energy, sapping their strength and draining them. The outlook was grim. General Halkett's request for relief was met with a stern reply by Wellington, 'Every Englishman on the field must die on the spot we now occupy.' For the Anglo-Allied army there were no reinforcements and no retreat. Irishmen of the 27th Foot, the Inniskillings, placed at the centre of Wellington's line just beyond the crossroads north of La Haye Sainte, were talking an unmerciful pummelling. It was a severe test, shattering their strength, causing ruinous death and injury. Within a short time, 16 of their 19 officers were killed or wounded, and some 493 of their 747 other ranks became casualties, a huge loss. But they did not break. They withstood the terrible torment of lead fired into flesh. Because they refused to move, they died where they stood, in square formation, so many that it was appallingly transformed in a horrifying manner to the starkly stunning sight of an almost 'dead square'. Died they did, in huge numbers, they were broken up, some literally blown into bits, but they did not break formation. Despite the onslaught of in-coming iron cannonballs and French skirmishers' musket balls, the remaining members of the 27th Foot courageously preserved their shape and stood their ground. The Irish battalion is one of the few British units memorialised on the battlefield of Waterloo. A simple stone erected in 1990 identifies the position that the 27th Foot, the Inniskillings, held during the battle and communicates a strong and dignified commentary on their bravery. The unit's ultimate successor, the end result of numerous downsizing, abolitions and amalgamations, the Royal Irish Regiment, has on ceremonial occasions symbolically maintained this memory in a now regimental tradition. With so many of the Inniskillings officers having been killed or wounded, the unit was commanded at the end of the fighting at Waterloo by its non-commissioned officer's instead, and so today on occasions the battalion is marched off the parade ground by these NCOs. 'Exposed...to all that came', is how Lieutenant Edward Drewe, himself with the 27th Foot, explained why they paid so grave a price. From his vantage point Captain Harry Ross-Lewin, 32nd Foot, although appalled, derived some little comfort in their distress, believing that his countrymen's horrible predicament nevertheless saw a display of 'a fine example of steadiness, discipline and passive courage,' which reflected well on all the Irish there. The ordeal of the Inniskillings at Waterloo, and the nerve with which they met it, is undoubtedly one of the better known chapters in an otherwise little known story of the Irish participation in the Waterloo campaign.

The noise, the smoke, the roars, the screams, the mud, the blood, and the madness; cannonballs and musket balls, slashing sabres and stabbing lances; heads and limbs smashed to smithereens, passive courage, acts of bravery, endurance and stoicism, were not experiences monopolised by the 27th Foot. The nearby 'Fighting Fortieth' (for its courage in Egypt 1800-02) were undergoing a not dissimilar 'painful and difficult experience'. Lieutenant Hugh Boyd Wray from County Laois recorded in his diary the loss suffered amongst his brother officers of the 40th Foot,

> Poor Fisher was hit, I was speaking to him, and I got all over his brains, his head was blown to atoms. Poor Major Heyland (who commanded) was shot (in) the heart, and poor Ford was shot thro' the spine of his back. Poor Clarke lost his left arm and I am much afraid Browne will lose his leg, he is shot thro' the upper part of the thigh and the bone terribly shattered. There are eight more of our officers wounded, but all are doing well except little Thornhill, who was wounded thro' the head.

Captain William Fisher had his head taken off by a cannon ball when standing near the colours. On one side of him was a Sergeant Lawrence, on the other, talking to him, was Lieutenant Hugh Boyd Wray. 'There goes my best friend,' exclaimed a private in Captain Fisher's Company. 'I will be as good a friend to you,' said Lieutenant Wray who immediately took the deceased's place in the square, unaware that Captain Fisher had ordered the man repeatedly flogged for slovenliness and was an old offender. He had spoken ironically, producing a grim laugh among the men, knowing what Lieutenant

Wray did not. It was just before then that Sergeant Lawrence was ordered to the 40th Foot's colours:

> There had been before me that day fourteen sergeants already killed and wounded while in charge of those colours, with officers in proportion, and the staff and colours were almost cut to pieces …I had not been there more than a quarter of an hour when a cannon-shot came and took the Captain's head clean off.

Shortly after, Major Arthur Heyland, from County Derry, officer commanding 40th Foot, was struck in the neck by a musket ball and died. The 40th Foot had been 300 yards behind the crucially important La Haye Sainte farmhouse defending the vital crossroads. In situ since three o'clock, they had been moved to there and had held firm against French cavalry attack and artillery bombardment. Now they were coping with the effects of the fall of the farmhouse, 'the crisis', so named because in the balance by the slimmest of threads hung the fate of the defence of Wellington's line. Captain Conyngham Ellis from Abbeyfeale, County Limerick, was doing his utmost to contribute to leading the 40th Foot's steadfast defence of the difficult exposed position.

Cut to pieces also was the 73rd (Highland) Regiment of Foot among whose ranks was Lieutenant Richard Leyne, from Tralee, County Kerry, son of Doctor Maurice Lyne. He had joined the 73rd Foot, bringing 400 volunteers from the 'Kerry Militia' and was rewarded with a lieutenancy. Because of the death and wounding of his fellow officers at Waterloo, he succeeded to the command of the regiment and kept it as long as the regiment was in France. But not before Major Dawson Kelly, County Armagh, a staff officer and an assistant quartermaster-general was approached by a sergeant of his (old) regiment who told him of the state of casualties amongst the officers of the 73rd Foot. Major Kelly immediately returned with

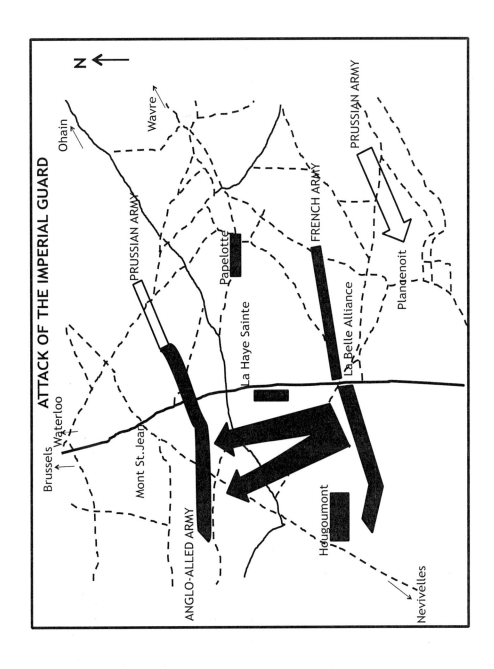

ATTACK OF THE IMPERIAL GUARD

the sergeant and took over command.

It was about this time, of all times, that the defence suffered the loss of an entire Hanoverian (German) battalion under Christian von Ompteda who received an order from the Prince of Orange, a 22-year-old general, to deploy his battalion in line and advance against French skirmishers who were ominously supported by French cavalry. Von Ompteda protested, but rather than admit his tactical mistake the prince insisted on his order being carried out, and the battalion perished uselessly, and at a crucial moment of all times! Matters looked bleak and were becoming increasingly so, particularly in the centre where the thinnest veneer of a defence were just about holding out. It was the most precarious moment in the battle for the Allies. Their line was open, vulnerable, and highly susceptible to a final French flourish. Any vigorously pursued push now would most likely have favourably dramatic results for the French. Marshal Ney sensed this and sought the infantry from Napoleon to drive the tantalisingly close victory home. Many things had gone wrong for Napoleon, and yet he was on the cusp of winning. Napoleon, the master of manoeuvre, had finally met Wellington, the diamond of defence. It was weight of numbers against master musketry, the brave and bold application of annihilation against the courageous ability to withstand attrition; it was where time was critical, and most crucially, it was time for the arrival of the Prussians.

The Prussians had begun to arrive and were pressing at Plancenoit in Napoleon's right rear, and he became hugely concerned about this, committing further troops to propping up his defence there. When Marshal Ney's messenger requested troops for the decisive push through at La Haye Sainte his reply was shaped by this distraction, 'Infantry, where am I to get it? Does he expect me to make it?' It was now seven o'clock and there was a full and frightening cacophony of gunfire all over the battlefield. At

Hougoumont, another attack was underway; at La Haye Sainte the centre of the ridge was being contested, and now the Prussians were becoming involved at Plancenoit. What Wellington needed was Prussians to arrive to the east of the ridge. Terrain, troops, and time, the three principal considerations uppermost in the minds of both Napoleon and Wellington, were all beginning to converge and intersect for a dramatic climax. From Napoleon's point of view there was still time to take the ridge before the Prussians arrived in strength to change the course of events. With the Prussians kept in check at Plancenoit, Napoleon ordered the Imperial Guard forward to the ridge.

On the Verge of Victory or Collapse? (The Attack of the Imperial Guard)

While Wellington was losing his capacity to defend, Napoleon was losing time to attack. Then at 7pm the Prussians lst Corps began to arrive near Wellington's left, allowing him to contract (shorten and strengthen) his line. The crisis was over, but the struggle still raged. Wellington brought Vivian's and Vandeleur's cavalry brigades from the left of his line to solidify his centre and move his last remaining far-right Dutch–Belgian reserves into his right-centre from Braine l'Alleud. Wellington was preparing for the assault he knew must come; he knew Napoleon would make one last effort to break his line. Thirty minutes later, at 7.30pm, the French Imperial Guard attacked.

'The fog and smoke lay so heavy and thick on the ground that we could only ascertain the approach of the enemy by the noise and clashing of arms which the French usually make in their advance,' wrote Major Dawson Kelly, 73rd Highlanders.

The Prussians had finally come to Waterloo in earnest. Their arrival towards the east of the ridge of Mont-St-Jean revived

Wellington's wavering lines, whose volumes of fire-power were growing thin, their desperate anxiety gripping deeper, but they had stood fast despite reaching a low ebb. That there was a line left at all for the Prussians to join had been a victory in itself. They had held the ridge for far longer than the plan had envisaged, but it was important now to turn that triumph into success. There was still hard fighting to be done, a battle to be won or lost, and with the French Imperial Guard coming directly to them, it was they who would have to do it.

Marshal Grouchy had not 'marched to the sound of the guns' but had adhered to Napoleon's earlier direction to stick close to Blücher's forces, the bulk of whom he mistakenly considered to be at Wavre. Neither had he received Napoleon's subsequent urgent instruction to join him at Waterloo. Those 33,000 troops and more than 90 cannons were not now available to Napoleon. Still he was confident, he was certain enough of victory to deploy his Imperial Guard for one last desperate gamble; after all, they had never before retreated in battle. In an effort to galvanise the slackening spirits of his own other troops, dispirited by the appearance of the Prussians, he dispatched a colonel to dispel this belief, instead to say this arrival of troops were Grouchy's, not the Prussians.

The final crushing blow was to be delivered by the Imperial Guard, somewhere between 4,500 and 6,000 of them marching with familiar conviction towards Wellington's centre. The first to engage them were the Anglo-Allied artillery. They had been in action all day, exposed both on the crest and its forward slope and so were themselves pounded by the Grand Battery and had not escaped unscathed. Among those remaining was Major Lloyd's artillery battery. Early in the morning, sometime around seven o'clock, they had taken their position on the right-centre of Wellington's line on the very crest of the slope in front of the 69th and 33rd Regiments of Foot. From the start the battery had suffered the full and ferocious effects of the French realigned Grand Battery before the French cavalry charges. Much of the battery had been blown to pieces, and there were moments when their ammunition had been expended and only reinforcements prevented their total destruction. Cuirassiers and lancers had charged through the battery repeatedly . Now they were active again and along with other Anglo-Allied artillery batteries were mercilessly pounding the advancing columns of the Imperial Guard, first with solid shot, then shell, and finally as they drew close, at 50 yards, canister. The rapidity and precision had a devastating effect, but notwithstanding the appalling death toll, large elements of the Guard reached the muzzles of Lloyd's and Cleeve's guns and for a time overran their positions. Having survived hostilities all day, now at the close of battle Major Lloyd was killed by a sword thrust delivered by an officer of the Guard, and Lieutenant William Harvey, County Wexford, lost his right arm.

The battle's crescendo had arrived, it had reached its high point, and with its culmination came another curious development. Why, instead of advancing against Wellington's weaker centre, Marshal Ney lead the Imperial Guard up the slope towards Wellington's centre-right has not ever been altogether made clear. Marshal Ney took command of the attack, having persuaded Napoleon on the advance that 'he was France' and that the Imperial dream must not die with him

Wellington's centre had suffered badly: the 32nd Foot had scarcely two officers and some 70 fighting troops left; the 27th Foot was practically decimated, and one of the few survivors, Private Thomas Kerrigan, was much later to die at Calky near Enniskillen in December 1862, having supposedly reached the ripe old age of 108. Meanwhile, the 73rd Foot were standing with just over ten per cent of their strength remaining. One of those was Maurice Shea from County Kerry, generally credited as being the last surviving British veteran of the Battle of Waterloo, dying in March 1892 at the age of 97. One Irishman who nearly did not survive was Lieutenant Colonel John Millet Hammerton, County Tipperary, officer commanding 44th Foot, who, having bravely led the 2nd Battalion, was first left for dead on that bloody field with several severe wounds in the head and thigh. A faithful non-commissioned officer, Sergeant Ryan, however, brought the wounded and insensible commander to the care of some skilful medical treatment. He slowly recovered, and with his devoted follower returned home to his country residence at Orchardstown, near Clonmel, County Tipperary. His place in command was taken by Major George O'Malley, Castlebar, County Mayo, who himself was twice wounded at Waterloo and had two horses shot under him. Meanwhile, the 40th Foot, now under the command of Captain Conyngham Ellis, Abbeyfeale, County Limerick, who had succeeded in the field Major Arthur Rowley Heyland, Castle Roe, County Derry, had taken a large number of casualties but was yet to take part in further action; before the battle was over they would have 167 killed and wounded.

The culmination of the day's fighting was at hand as the first of the Imperial Guard columns swept over the ridge. They found it littered with corpses but bereft of any live occupants. The Imperial Guard had advanced in five columns which saw them merge into two echelons each, the fifth taking up a covering position at the foot of the slope. They were to arrive separately but altogether en masse, moving individually down the slope's reverse side. Visibility was limited due to the lingering smoke. As the forward column of the Imperial Guard appeared, the Brunswickers in Wellington's line broke as did d'Aubremes Brigade, and it looked very much as if the final all-out assault by the Guard would succeed. However, the volley of shots from Halkett's Brigade, who were four deep in line, an alternative formation to the square, was fierce in the extreme, having been fired at 50 yards. The attack of the first column wavered. Major Dawson Kelly, 73rd Regiment of the Foot, described the moment,

They kept up a confused and running fire, which we did not reply to, until they reached nearly a level with us, when a well-directed volley put them into confusion from which they did not appear to recover, but after a short interval of musketry on both sides, they turned about to a man and fled.

Meanwhile the other column that had previously advanced and was astonished to find nothing in front of them became far more astounded when Maitland's brigade of guards, previously instructed by Wellington to lie down, suddenly, on order, stood up, all I, 500 of them, and poured volley after volley into the Imperial Guard. They too became unsteady and undecided, their confidence deserting them until they suddenly stopped, staggered and became convulsed in disorder. Never before had they failed in an attack.

As this was happening the last echelon of the Imperial Guard hit Wellington's line. The 52nd Foot – which included Captain John Cross, Darton, County Armagh, Lieutenant the Honourable William Browne, third son of Valentine, 5th Viscount Kenmare, Ensign William Nettles, County Cork, who was killed carrying the King's colours, and County Wexford brothers Robert and Thomas Freeman – was commanded by Lieutenant Colonel Colborne, who astutely assessed the advancing column to be unlike that of D'Erlon's columns earlier in the day, for these were narrower and deeper, so the best way to get more effect – if you like, to kill more Frenchmen – was not so much to overlap them by line from the front, but to outflank them. Consequently, he marched his battalion down their flank, turned them inwards, and opened fire. The projection of thousands of heavy leaden musket balls engulfed the French who were caught in a narrow column and unable to respond with anything near the same weight of fire. But try they did, and an exchange of fire erupted at 50 yards. The confrontation continued for just five minutes but at great cost: the 52nd lost 150 men, and the French many more as their formation was ripped apart.

All along 'the line of contact' the French Imperial Guard had been sensationally stunned to a stupor by skilful, largely British, battle-craft and superior weapon-handling from a defence that stood steady. The French in their dazed condition were highly susceptible to an onslaught by bayonet charge. Once recognised, the opportunity was immediately seized upon, and as the Anglo-Allied infantry surged forward, the French gave way. Neither was the chance to augment the opportunity lost on the remnants of the British cavalry who cascaded forward in a full torrent. Sir de Lacey Evans described what happened, 'As we approached at a moderate pace the fronts and flanks began to turn their backs inwards; the rear of the columns had already begun to run away.' The French attack had been stopped and was now been driven back in its entirety. With fixed bayonets, Captain Conyngham Ellis's 40th Foot charged forward in the general advance and helped recapture La Haye Sainte farmhouse. As a reward for their steadfastness the 40th Regiment of Foot were later permitted to encircle their badge with a wreath of laurels.

Maintaining the pressure on the retreating French among the brilliant charge of Vivian and Vandeleur's cavalry were the 18th Hussars. Initially positioned on the extreme left (east) of Wellington's line, they had been one of the first units to encounter the arrival of the Prussian troops of Blücher's army as they started to converge on Mont-St-Jean. The previous charge of the 'Drogheda Cossacks', the Irish light cavalry regiment, was described by its commander, Lieutenant Colonel Henry Murray, as a costly action that 'had been attended with casualty but retiring (afterwards) proved infinitely more destructive. In returning there was a party of men with me at first, so many fell I do not think another man remained.' Now, on the forward foot, it was time to reverse the fortunes and this was attended to without hesitation. Joining this offensive action was Lieutenant Colonel John Dawson, Earl of Portarlington, officer commanding the 23rd Light Dragoons, who had earlier in the battle been absent from where his duty required him to be. In the interim he had arrived to the field of battle and wholeheartedly partook in the 18th Hussar's destructive and successful charge made now at the close of battle. He did so with great courage and even had a horse shot out from under him. However, his earlier non-appearance was to cause him great personal anguish in his later life, his remorse weighing heavily upon him, to the extent he was unable to outgrow it, living and dying in much reduced circumstance. Reported absent also by the editor of the *Military Calendar* was Irishman Lieutenant Colonel Patrick Doherty, 13th Hussars (Light Dragoons), stated to be lying ill at Brussels, suffering from a severe attack of West Indian fever. (Present on 16 and 17 June, he received the Waterloo medal). His place was taken by Major Shetland Boyse of New Ross, County Wexford. Colonel's Doherty's son, George, a lieutenant with the 13th Hussars, had a noteworthy happening: having taken out his watch to see the time he did not have time to put it away properly when the order to advance was given so he instead put it into the breast of his jacket where it prevented a musket ball penetrating and thus saved his life. He was, however, later severely wounded in the head at Waterloo but survived to live on for 20 years, dying in Dublin. Another survivor of the regimental charge was Lieutenant John H. Drought from Letterbrook, County Offaly.

Also in cavalry action that day was Lieutenant Standish Darby O'Grady, County Limerick, 7th Hussars, afterwards Colonel

Viscount Guillamore, aide-de-camp to the Queen. He had been stationed on the ground above Hougoumont on the Anglo-Allied right. He wrote a letter to his father just after the battle,

> The 7th had an opportunity of showing what they could do if they got fair play. We charged twelve or fourteen times, and once cut off a squadron of cuirassiers every man of whom we killed on the spot except the two officers and one Marshal de Laoi, whom I sent to the rear.

His sister was Margaret O'Grady who married William Harrison of Cork. William's sister was mother of Lieutenant William (Harrison) Harvey.

The counter-attack and cavalry charge drove the French from the field. The attack of the Imperial Guard was over. The Battle of Waterloo was over. The Napoleonic War was over. The pursuit of the retreating French by the Prussians continued,. Thereafter the Anglo-Allies continued into France to reach Paris. The desperate heroism of the Anglo-Allied resistance, no better exemplified than by the solid stoicism of the 27th Foot, the 'Inniskillings', won the day for Wellington, together with Wellington's defensive talents and tactics, his troops' tenacity, Blücher's arrival, and Napoleon's mistakes; even the weather had contributed to the victory. The next day Wellington wrote to his brother William,

It was the most desperate business I was ever in. I never took so much trouble about any battle, & never was so near being beat. Our loss is immense particularly in the best of all instruments, British Infantry. I never saw the Infantry behave so well.

Using time talent, opportunity and experience, Wellington had masterminded, led, and seized upon each moment to skilfully orchestrate a victory from a difficult situation. In what was one of the greatest battles of all time, the Irish played a significant role, perhaps even tipping the balance, by warding off the disintegration of Wellington's line when it was on the verge of collapse. As Home Secretary Henry Addington, 1st Viscount Sidmouth, wrote on June 24 1815, 'It is not too much to assert, that the supply of troops derived from Ireland turned to the scale on the 18th of June at Waterloo...'

THE AFTERMATH

'Much Execution'

THE DESPERATION of Napoleon's driving ambition, denied by as desperate a defence against it, saw 'much execution' exercised, many lives cut short, others horribly ruined. Waterloo's shocking intensity witnessed the cruel destruction of lives, brutal infliction of wounds, and troops 'doing murder' to each other. Civilisation had fallen down and humanity descended into darkness. The aftermath of the day's battle was a clear, cold, moonlit night barely concealing a sickening sight, the dead unburied, the wounded unattended. The battle's end had been abrupt, the outcome clear cut, with dusk immediately descending to hurriedly draw a curtain across a grim scene. Unusually, the victors remained on the field, the living among or near the dead and the dying. Shocked survivors were drained and exhausted and those lucky to be deafened by cannon and musket fire could not hear the pitiful pleas of the wounded for water and the heart-rendering, pathetic cries of the dying pleading to be saved from their plight. Some begged to be put out of their misery, others clung on to life, craving attention, while all around could be heard, groans, shrieks, and shouts. Some would somehow survive, cheating death, while others silently succumbed to their wounds in the cold of the night, lying next to those already dead, some with no wounds apparent.

Many died needlessly for the want of being attended to, while others received the unwelcome attentions of fellow humans whose sole motivation was self-enrichment, the plunderers and scavengers. Fellow soldiers ransacked the remains of those whom they had fought against, and even in some cases with, pillaging what they could, money, watches, rings, rank markings, boots, badges, buckles, uniforms, spectacles, teeth even, sometimes cold-heartedly stabbing to death those wounded who were reluctant to give up their valuables.

Waterloo was won, losses were large, the battlefield small. The ghastly aftermath of the battle saw strewn across the whole field a mass of dead bodies, men and horses, some literally piled on each other. The day's whirlwind, a vortex of violence, resulted in a shocking casualty count: one in every four combatants killed or wounded. The mortality rate was extraordinary, in so far as it is possible to estimate, and many approximations are judgement calls. In round figures, Wellington lost 15,000 men, Blücher 7,000, and Napoleon 30,000, a total of 52,000, gauged to be 25 per cent of the total number of combatants on the field. The totality of the figure tells its own story but does not tell of the individual experiences of the those who made up that colossal figure, one of the most unique being that of Irishman the Honourable Lieutenant Colonel Frederick Ponsonby, officer commanding the 12th Regiment of Light Dragoons. A second cousin of Major General Sir William Ponsonby, he was involved in the charge of Major General Ponsonby's cavalry brigade in the early afternoon, repelling the attack of the massed French infantry:

> Nothing could equal the confusion of this melee, as we had succeeded in destroying and putting to flight the infantry. I

was anxious to withdraw my Regiment, but almost at the same moment I was wounded in both arms, my horse sprung forward and carried me to the rising ground on the right of the French position, where I was knocked off my horse by a blow on the head.

It then fell to junior Captain (later Colonel) Sampson Stawell, Kilbrittain Castle, County Cork, 'to bring the regiment out of action at Waterloo after all its senior officers had been killed or wounded'. The Stawells were an interesting family, as Captain Stawell's father, a colonel in the Bandon cavalry, was sympathetic to the United Irishmen, and it is said that he persuaded the local United Irishmen in the area not to rise up as Bandon was too heavily garrisoned for them to succeed there; that they should await to hear what was happening in Wexford, to where a large contingent of troops stationed around Bandon as a result of the attempted French invasion at Bantry in 1796 had departed. Sampson Stawell represented Kinsale in Parliament and his residence in London was at the United Services Club, London. He had a nephew, 17-year-old Coronet Henry Boyle Bernard, 1st Regiment of Dragoon Guards, who was also at Waterloo and was the fifth son of Francis Bernard and Catherine Boyle of Castle Bernard Bandon, burnt down by the IRA in 1921 during Ireland's War of Independence

Meanwhile, Lieutenant Colonel Fredrick Ponsonby, recovering from his brief state of unconsciousness, began to stir himself and was noticed by a passing French lancer. Struggling to regain his balance, Ponsonby heard the lancer exclaim 'Tu n'est pas mort, coquin' (You're not dead, you rascal) and thrust his lance through his back. 'My head dropped, the blood gushed into my mouth, a difficulty of breathing came on, and I though all was over.'

It was not long before a *tirailleur* (French skirmisher) paid him unwanted attention, manhandling him coarsely and robbing him of his money. Still unable to defend himself, he was once again put upon by another seeking plunder. And yet a third visitor, this time a compassionate French officer, giving him brandy, placed a knapsack under his head and turned him on his side to make what he supposed would be his last hours more comfortable, then passed on 'to pursue the retreating British'. The battle raged around him but his own drama continued. 'Presently another tirailleur appeared, who came and knelt and fired over me, loading and firing many times, and conversing with great gaiety all the while. At last he ran off.' Evening arrived and with the close of battle came the Prussians. 'Two squadrons of Prussian cavalry, both of them two deep, passed over me at full trot, lifting me up from the ground and tumbling me about cruelly.' Darkness descended and he became aware of a wounded man lying across his legs and yet another presence. 'A German soldier bent on plunder came and pulled me about roughly before he left me.' At midnight a British soldier appeared and hauled the wounded soldier off Ponsonby's legs, secured a sword, and stood sentry over him until dawn. With six wounds, a punctured lung, having lain wounded for 18 hours, he was placed in a cart and removed to a farmhouse. Lieutenant Colonel Ponsonby survived his wounds, the looters, plunders, and scavengers who were thick on the ground that night, and who even robbed each other, killing each other if they had to. Later on these prowlers would be the local peasants, but for now they dared not venture out.

Plundering of the enemy's dead was a practice generally engaged in, the richer pickings of course found on the bodies of officers, by those hard-hearted enough to carry out such deeds. All told, among the collective dead of those fatally wounded officers a small fortune lay out in the moonlit battlefield of Waterloo. Their personal weapons were worth money to the scavengers: pistols and swords, epaulettes and gold braid, and of course their personal effects – purses, watches, telescopes, perhaps rings and individual keepsakes and ornamental mementos. If greed stimulated those sufficiently daring to brave the risky undertaking of looting during the night, there were those who had a far stronger motivation which compelled them out on to the grisly field of death. Accompanying dependants, albeit few in number, had travelled to Belgium either officially or unofficially. Captain Alexander Cavalié Mercer, Royal Horse Artillery, when disembarking at Ostend, Belgium, two months previously noted and remarked on the presence of some Irish camp followers:

> Disconsolate-looking groups of women and children were to be seen in search of their husbands, or mayhap of a small child, all clamouring, lamenting, and materially increasing the babel-like confusion, amidst which Erin's brogue was everywhere predominant.

There were many Irish among the dead and wounded, and once battle had been joined the fate of loved ones was once again uncertain. There were those who undertook in person the fraught search for their husbands. Irish woman Jenny Jones (maiden name, Griffiths) married to Private Lewis Jones, a Welshman in the 23rd Foot, had travelled to Belgium with the British army and at battle's end sought out the fate of her husband. This involved a frantic search of the battlefield. She eventually found him wounded after an anguishing hunt through a scene of great slaughter. Private Jones recovered and he and his wife settled in Wales on his discharge from the army.

There were three privates by the name McMullen (Peter, John, and William) who served with the 1st battalion of the 27th Inniskillings ('The Skins') and received the Waterloo Medal, but one of them, Peter, from a weaving background in Downpatrick, also received the anxious attentions of the formidable Mrs Elisabeth McMullen who when he fell seriously wounded, herself heavily pregnant, dragged him from the battlefield, receiving a musket ball in the leg in the process. After receiving medical attention they were both hospitalised in Antwerp. Elisabeth benefited greatly from the rest and her wounded leg healed, but Peter lost both his arms. Transferred to a hospital in Chelsea, London, Elisabeth gave birth to a daughter. When news of her bravery came to the attention of the Commander-in-Chief of the British Army, the Duke of York, he paid a personal visit to the hospital and agreed to became sponsor to the infant girl, who was subsequently christened Frederica McMullen Waterloo.

Very nearly among the wounded was Wellington himself. Having been almost constantly within range of enemy fire throughout most of the day, he nonetheless remained unflappable even when those within close proximity fell to cannon and musket fire, most notably Lord Uxbridge, his overall cavalry commander and unofficial second-in-command, who had his left leg blown off while seated on his horse immediately next to Wellington.

The battle fought, there was a victor and a vanquished. At the battle's end, Wellington briefly met Blücher at La Belle Alliance, and the two commanders greeted each other as victor. Drained mentally, exhausted emotionally, Wellington was of course nevertheless hugely relieved. Now dark, having ridden back across the battlefield, he dismounted from his chestnut horse Copenhagen and giving him a friendly pat on his rear quarter was startled when Copenhagen uncharacteristically lashed out with a hind hoof narrowly missing Wellington's head. Wellington had two narrow escapes at Waterloo.

It has been sometimes suggested that both Copenhagen and Napoleon's horse, Marengo, were purchased at Cahirmee horse fair near Buttevant County Cork, an annual fair that continues up to the present day. Cahirmee is considered to be among the oldest horse fairs in Europe and while its claims to be ancient rings true, it is highly doubtful that either Copenhagen or Marengo changed owners there.

Unknown, however, was the name of the horse that carried the also anonymous but evidently beautiful French female rider in cavalry officer's uniform, who was found among the dead on the ridge just below the much fought over crossroads at Waterloo. A participant of an earlier cavalry charge, she had seen 'much execution' that day, until she too became a victim to it.

'Saw Bones'

Dulled by excessive employment, the surgeon's instruments quickly lost their sharpened edge and became blunt. A saw for amputation, a scalpel for bleeding, a forceps for extraction of musket balls, a drill for trepanning, splints for fractures, an array of knives to assist with all this and more, the surgeon's instrument case closely resembled a tradesman's toolbox. They had neither anaesthetics nor antiseptics, and there were neither field ambulances nor field hospitals. At Waterloo medical treatment was rudimentary, techniques crude, conditions basic, infection common. That is how it was and how it was expected to be. The butchery of the battlefield was matched by the rawness and scientific paucity of the practices and procedures to deal with it.

> The mangled bodies of men and horses, broken gun – carriages, caps, helmets, cuirasses, arms, drums, harness, accoutrements, pieces of battered uniforms, knapsacks, letters, and cards, that were strewed abundantly in all directions, and the caps levelled by the trampling of infantry and cavalry in the strife, plainly marked the extent of the field, and gave undeniable evidence of the fury of the conflict that had raged there. – *Captain Harry Ross-Lewin, 19 June 1815, County*

Clare 32nd Foot

'The fury of the conflict' caused an unprecedented number of casualties for a battle of that era. Those who were carried from the battlefield and those who could walk to medical aid stations in nearby barns and cottages had already overwhelmed the capacity of the medical capability available, and there were thousands more lying both unattended to, and undiscovered, throughout the battlefield.

> Two Irish light – infantry men sending forth such howlings and wailings, and oaths and excretions, as were shocking to hear. One of them had his leg shot off the other his thigh smashed by a cannon-shot. They were certainly pitiable objects.– *Captain Cavalié Mercer, Royal Horse Artillery*

It was such 'pitiable objects' that Surgeon James O'Malley from Castlebar, County Mayo, 11th Regiment of Light Dragoons, and brother of George O'Malley, 44th Foot, along with the other battalion and regimental surgeons and assistant surgeons had to save after the day-long jarring bloodshed. The majority of wounds was caused by the low-velocity, three-quarter-inch lead musket ball, cannon ball impact or blast, and gaping slash wounds from bladed weapons and lances. Bleeding, shock, thirst, exposure, and infection were additional complications compounding the wounds if unattended to. Lying out on the battlefield for two days and three nights before being discovered and treated was Troop Sergeant Major Matthew Marshall, Enniskillen, 6th Dragoons, with 19 wounds;, amazingly he survived. Lieutenant John Roberts, County Antrim, 71st Foot, received a grape-shot wound from a metal fragment weighing 10 ounces, which he kept as a relic, hooped in silver. The shot entered at the breast and was cut out at the shoulder three days later. When Lieutenant Colonel Frederick Ponsonby eventually reached the surgeons he was subjected, in accordance with the prevailing medical wisdom of the period, to a strict regime of bleeding, 120 ounces in two days; he lived until 1837. Lieutenant John Browne, County Mayo, 4th Foot, while leading his company, received a fearful wound from a bullet over the ear and fell senseless. He was left on the field for dead and was reported killed. His family in Ireland went into mourning for him. However, he recovered by trepanning (drilling to remove the musket ball and relieve the pressure) and continued to serve, living until 1849.

Hugely overwhelmed by the numbers requiring treatment, surgeons with rolled-up sleeves remained busy for days, forwarding on causalities by cart over rough cobblestone roads to hospitals and churches, barracks, and other buildings improvised as medical and posts. As these were already overflowing, the wounded had to be laid out on straw in the city's squares. Edward Costello, County Laois, 95th Rifles, described the scene:

> The scene surpassed all imagination, and baffles description: thousands of wounded French, Belgians, Prussians and English; carts, wagons, and every other available vehicle, were continually arriving heaped with sufferers. The wounded were laid, friends and foes indiscriminately, on straw, with avenues between them, in every part of the city, and nearly destitute of surgical attendance. The humane and indefatigable exertions of the fair ladies of Brussels however, greatly made up for this deficiency ; numbers were busily employed – some strapping and bandaging wounds, other serving out tea, coffee, soups, and other soothing nourishments.

Amputation needed to be performed as swiftly as possibly. Infections, sepsis, and gangrene in particular, were not well understood by medical men of the time. Shock was always a possible fatal side-effect, causing the vital organs to cease functioning because of the dropping of blood pressure. Those with mangled limbs deemed necessary for amputation, such as Lieutenant William Harvey, County Wexford, and Ensign Edward Hodder, Fountainstown, County Cork, 69th Foot, would be held down by the surgeon's assistants on a table, bench or sturdy surface, given a sharp swallow of gin or rum for anaesthetic, and have a leather strap placed between their teeth to bite on. An insertion was made in the flesh above the wound by a knife with a curve-shaped blade and the exposed bone sawn through. Needle and thread next, as first the arteries were sewn up and then the excess piece of the skin from above the wound sewn over the stump and then all cauterized by tar to stop the bleeding and prevent infection. It was not terribly technical and it did not take long. It was an elementary procedure, mechanical even, and certainly barbaric by today's standards, but it was frequently successful, with well over half surviving the experience.

The cannon shot that was removed from the leg of Edward Hodder. The paper around the centre has been left in place as it has been inscribed with the details.

Major Edmund L' Estrange, County Offaly, 71st Foot, ADC to Sir Denis Pack, was one for whom it did not work. His right leg shattered by a round shot (cannon ball), he died soon after undergoing amputation. He had served in the Peninsular War and his actions on several occasions attracted the attention of Wellington. During the war he was captured by the French and was held as a prisoner of war at Verdun. He was a brevet major at the young age of 26. He had a remarkable but short career. A less dramatic, more lingering example of the ill effects of amputation may be seen in the case of Ensign William Aldworth Clarke, Cork City, 40th Foot. He died in Sterling in December 1827, twelve and a half years after the battle, from complications arising from the loss of his left arm at Waterloo; he had been apparently plagued by health problems from 1815 onwards.

The removal of musket balls was done with a probe, the surgeon's finger, which would be pushed into the wound and the musket ball located, after which a specially shaped forceps would extract the lead. Unless it had hit a critical organ, the chances of survival were good as long as no material or dirt was not left in the wound that would later cause it to become gangrenous.

The well-practised procedure of bleeding, the taking of blood from the body by leaking it or by applying leeches, was much believed in but had absolutely no scientific basis whatsoever, and patients like Lieutenant Colonel Frederick Ponsonby, commanding officer, 12th Light Dragoons, survived in spite of, not because of, such treatment.

There had never been a battle like Waterloo, fought over 15 square kilometres, with 180,000 participants, leading to a huge casualty count and high concentration of dead and wounded. Struggling as they were in its aftermath to cope with the volumes of the wounded, they also had to deal with the huge numbers of dead.

They were buried and burned over the next eight to ten days with a large number of locals employed to clear the field. By the month's end there was little left except a lingering stench of death. The battle was over, but the battle to prevent the wounded joining the dead went on, the tragedy being that many who survived their wounds or amputations succumbed in recovery because of the surroundings in which they lay; non-ventilated premises meant men died not just from sepsis and gangrene, but of disease quickly spreading in the over-crowded, oxygen-starved conditions in which they lay.

For three days immediately after the battle the surgeons (the 'saw bones') worked tirelessly to tend to the immense quantity of wounded men. Even after that, wounded men continued to be discovered on the field. Surgeons arrived from England to assist in the ad hoc hospitals that sprung up around the city, with the established hospitals already overflowing. As distinguished Irish staff surgeon John Mennon remarked of the Gendarmerie hospital,

> Three hundred men were collected in this hospital, the majority desperately, not to say incurable, wounded. Among them were one hundred and forty compound fractures, viz. 86 of the thigh, 48 of the leg and 6 of the arm. They had been collected all over the country by the peasantry, and dragged from barn to barn, often without food or dressings and did not arrive to Brussels until various periods from the 8th to the 13th day after they were wounded.

He was also to write, 'Assuredly no body of men ever laboured harder in the cause of humanity than the British surgeons after the battle of Waterloo.'

The trauma of the battle was not easily recovered from, even for those who were victorious and not wounded. The experience of Waterloo was an emotional shock to the system, powerfully agonizing and painful. Typically, the stress was seldom articulated, but one month after the battle Wellington wrote to Frances Lady Shelley, a woman with whom he had some acquaintance,

> While in the thick of it, I am much too occupied to feel anything; but it is wretched after. It is quite impossible to think of glory. Both mind and feelings are exhausted. I am wretched even at the moment of victory, and I always say that next to a battle lost, the greatest misery is a battle gained. Not only do you lose those dear friends with whom you have been living, but you are forced to leave the wounded behind you. To be sure one tries to do the best for them, but how little that is ! At such moments every feeling in your breast is deadened. I am now just beginning to retain my natural spirits, but I never wish for any more fighting.

The Battle of Waterloo was a 'bloody day' and memories of it being so remained forever with those who survived, both victor and vanquished.

Celebration and Commemoration

ASIA AND EUROPE SAVED BY THEE,
PROCLAIM INVINCIBLE IN WAR, THY DEATHLESS NAME.
NOW ROUND THY BROW CIVIL OAK WE TWINE,
THAT EVERY EARTHY GLORY MAY BE THINE.
– *Wellington Monument, Phoenix Park, Dublin*

Wellington's victory at Waterloo brought a definite conclusion to the struggle against Revolutionary and Napoleonic France. There had been two decades of war, followed by a brief period of peace, then no peace after Napoleon's escape from Elba and the 'Hundred Days' campaign, but now, finally, real peace. The victory at had brought the recognition that an exceptional happening had occurred, and this reverberated around Europe. There was enormous reassurance

Royal Hospital Kilmainham.

and relaxation after much anxiety and apprehension. There was cause, if ever there was cause, for an outpouring of celebration and commemoration, and that is what happened.

The victory had a discernible impact in Ireland. The Irish connections to the campaign had involved the country effectively functioning as a large staging post for the campaign; and because of the specific Irish personalities who took part, the military units of explicit Irish affiliation and the fact that Irishmen formed a large portion of the rest of the Anglo-allied army, the celebrations were widespread throughout the country. A subscription fund for the relief and benefit of the Irish families of the brave men killed was well supported.

This euphoria also gave rise to a significant demand for detailed reportage of the events, with the publishing of Wellington's famous

The Wellington Monument in the Phoenix Park, Dublin.

despatch providing the first full account of the happenings. Personal letters home by participants to their families became an additional source. Later, first-hand verbal accounts from 'those who were there' during periods of leave home also helped fill the void, allowing, for example, Captain Harry Ross-Lewin, County Clare, 'to tell long stories to my friends'.

Wellington's force remained in France as an army of occupation so there was neither one single mass return of units nor large-scale victorious home comings into Ireland. Eager to give expression to the emotions and passions that the victory inspired, a plethora of plays, poems, paintings and songs animated that joyous sense which captivated the public. The Irish painter Thomas Story was one of the very first artists to arrive at the scene of the battle, capturing in watercolour scenes of Waterloo, Mont-St-Jean and Quatre Bras two and three days after the hostilities. Thereafter many curious sightseers were drawn to the battlefield to view for themselves the site of the 'terrible action'. Many of these early battlefield tourists found themselves being offered for purchase 'relics of the field' by local Belgians: French 'eagle' cap badges, cuirasses, sabres, bayonets, and other 'spoils of war'. Occasionally the battleground offered up more grisly relics, even many years after, one such as late as 1906 with the discovery of the body of Lieutenant Michael McClusky, 6th Inniskilling Dragoons, killed during the charge of the British Henry Cavalry Brigade. For those who could not or did not go to Waterloo, the battlefield, as it were, came to them, in the form of the 'Waterloo Panorama' which was put on show near Dublin's Eden Quay. Ten thousand square feet of canvas depicted nine different 'interesting periods of the battle' with life-size figures. The panorama's run had to be extended due to overwhelming public demand.

An eagerness began for naming streets and other landmarks after the battle. Dublin's iconic cast-iron arched pedestrian bridge, widely known to-day as the 'Half-Penny Bridge', but officially called 'The Liffey Bridge', was named 'Wellington Bridge' when it was built in 1816. Waterloo and Wellington Roads, avenues, terraces and places in Dublin and other Irish cities owe their titles to this era, as does the largest obelisk in Europe. Standing at 62 metres (203 feet) tall, this pillar began its construction in 1817 in the south-east of Dublin's Phoenix Park. Designed by Sir Robert Smirke, its progress was halted in 1820 due to a shortage of money and it was not completed until 1861. Because it was built while Wellington was still alive it was called the 'Wellington Testimonial', more commonly referred to today as the Wellington Monument. It celebrates the victories of Wellington in four bronze plaques on the bottom part of the monument, one of them titled 'Waterloo' by the Irish sculptor Sir Thomas Farrell.

Built 131 years before the Battle of Waterloo, across the River Liffey, is one of the oldest and finest 17th century classic public buildings in Ireland, the Royal Hospital Kilmainham. With its formal façade and large courtyard, its design was not unlike Les Invalides in Paris, which in its time saw housed some of Ireland's 'Wild Geese' who had seen military service with French armies. The Royal Hospital was built in the ruins of the medieval hospital and monastery of the Knights of Saint John of Jerusalem (Knights Hospitaller). This building, founded by Strongbow in 1174, replaced the 7th century Christian settlement of Cill Maighneamn from which Kilmainham gets its name. Today the Irish Museum of Modern Art (IMMA) is located there. The Royal Hospital Chelsea in London was a sister Institution to the Royal Hospital Kilmainham, both having the remit of providing some comfort, peace, and security in their later years to those who had given service in the British military. With a capacity to house 250, the Royal Hospital Kilmainham often housed more. It cost £36,500 to build, its construction and running costs met by a levy on soldiers' pay, initially twelve, then reduced to six, pence per week. The Royal Hospital would grant admission in due course to veterans of Waterloo. Here, some of those whose service contributed to the great victory of 18 June 1815 lived out their final days, and some when they died were interred internally in the burial ground for soldiers immediately adjacent to 'Bully's Acre', one of Dublin's oldest cemeteries. Among the more than 300 buried there is Corporal James Graham from County Monaghan, Coldstream Guards, who had fought so bravely at the château of Hougoumont.

Illuminations, subscription funds to support families of those killed at Waterloo, monuments erected to notable participants of the battle, panoramas, plays, paintings, poems, the naming of streets, structures, and other places, and the writing of accounts of personal involvement were all activities undertaken both in the immediate

Sergeant James Graham (in Pensioner Uniform, Royal
Hospital Kilmainham), National Gallery of Ireland.

aftermath of the battle and for a long time afterwards. One interesting initiative was the construction of a highly detailed model of the battle. Completed in Ireland in 1838 after eight years of meticulous research by Captain William Siborne, it involved an eight-month survey of the battlefield and obtaining extensive information from mostly British officers on the positions of their troops at the time of the battles 'crisis' prior to 7pm. Costing three thousand pounds to construct, it was shipped from Ireland in 39 sections, re-assembled, and put on public display in the Egyptian Hall, Piccadilly, London. Although it was a big success, attracting approximately 100,000 visitors who paid a shilling entry fee, the project ran into serious debt. On its return to Ireland in 1841 it was placed in storage until a subscription was raised by British regiments depicted in the battle to purchase the model, and it was once again displayed in London, this time in the Banqueting Hall, Whitehall, as part of the Royal United Services Museum, until finally being presented to the National Army Museum in Chelsea. The by-product of the model's making, nearly 700 first-hand accounts, which were replies to Captain Siborne's circular letter used as the basis for the detail of its construction, became a unique archive and the sound basis for a contribution to his history of the Waterloo campaign published in 1844. Captain Siborne was appointed secretary and adjutant of the Royal Military Asylum at Chelsea in late 1843, in which appointment he remained until his death.

The celebratory mood in the immediate aftermath of the battle was tempered temporarily by the unlikely effects of a far-away occurrence. Simultaneous to the eruption of war in Europe was the actual physical eruption of the Tampora volcano in Indonesia. Killing hundreds of thousands in its immediate vicinity, its ash cloud caused a cooling of the temperatures in far-off Europe, Ireland included, and even north America. This phenomenon adversely affected wheat growth and caused much harm to harvests, leading to food shortages and hardship. The ill-effects of this natural occurrence were, of course, short-lived; lingering for longer was the dividend of victory over Napoleon, peace in Europe. This, however, was not without consequence in Ireland. War in Europe, continuous for over 20 years, had been good for those involved in the supply of goods and services to the British military. The cessation of war meant a serious downturn in the activities of all those connected, which many in Ireland were as the country had been a prominent staging post for British troops departing for campaigns abroad. This did not cease altogether, however; indeed with Napoleon's aspirations finally dealt with, the further enlargement of the British Empire

The Waterloo Medal.

could continue unimpeded, at least from the French. Ireland had then to decrease and moderate the extent of its involvement as a staging post; now its direction and degree was driven by the eventful episodes of British expeditionary expansion and enforcement.

These economic adjustments and other very real direct effects of victory over Napoleon could not negate the joy of the very fact of having defeated him in the first place. Peace had now to be faced, indeed embraced – a far, far better alternative to war.

An 'Honourable Badge'

'The Prince Regent has been graciously pleased, in the name and on behalf of his Majesty, to command that, in commemoration of the brilliant and decisive victory of Waterloo, a medal should be conferred to every officer, non-commissioned officer, and soldier of the British army present upon that memorable occasion, etc.' This 'Waterloo Medal' was given to every man present on three days, namely, Quatre Bras 16 June 1815, action on the 17 June 1815, and Waterloo 18 June 1815.

Of the 39,000 medals issued, about 6,000 went to the cavalry units, 4,000 to the guards, 16,000 to the infantry/foot units, 5,000 to the artillery, 6,500 to the King's German Legion, and 1,500 to miscellaneous units. Its introduction was not without controversy as these who had participated in campaigns other than Waterloo were disgruntled. The resentment was eventually resolved much later in 1847 when a Military General Service Medal was instituted retrospectively, recognising campaign service from 1793 to 1814. Many of the recipients of the Waterloo Medal were to look upon it as a prized possession, marking as it did the very first time that the British army awarded a general campaign medal, an acknowledgement of the importance of the victory at Waterloo. An 'Honourable Badge' is how Corporal Edward Costello described his decoration, a silver medal with a depiction of Britain's Prince Regent (later King George IV) on its front face and the goddess Victory's representation on the reverse side, suspended from a crimson ribbon with blue edging. On display today at the Royal Hospital Kilmainham is the 'Waterloo Medal' of former Private Charles Hall, County Fermanagh, 32nd Foot, who died as a pensioner there in December 1878, He bequeathed this medal to the Royal Hospital in grateful appreciation of the attention he received there in his old age.

The participants at Waterloo were also recipients of official 'prize money'. 'The captured French 'baggage train' and other war 'reparations'were a tangible reward shared proportionately according to rank by those who had served during the Waterloo campaign. At the time when a soldier's pay was a shilling a day minus deductions for food, clothing, and other necessities, his net pay into his hand was often less than half of that. So with 12 pennies making a shilling, and 20 shillings a pound, the prize money awarded to an infantry private for his participation in the Waterloo campaign was nearly the net equivalent of a month's pay. The appropriate proportion for lieutenant was £35. Ensign James Harvey,County Wexford, Coldstream Guards, one of the party that closed the North Gate at Hougoumont, received 34 pounds, 14 shillings, 9½ pennies as Prize Money on 11 August (he was retired on half-pay on 15 April 1819).

For service for a set number of years in the military, a soldier received a pension, an income not enjoyed by many during and after the Napoleonic wars. Length of service determined eligibility for the right to receive this settlement. Waterloo veterans were accorded two years' service time extra for pension purposes. Then as now, with pension more important than pay, this was a valuable and meaningful award.

The benefit of peace is the absence of war, and with the threat of hostilities ended, so too the need for a large standing army. Wellington loved his army and, recognising the signs, hid it. He kept intact as much of the army as he could by deploying as much as he could of it overseas, out of the public eye and consciousness. Despite these anticipatory actions much of the army was indeed disbanded, downsized, and amalgamated, so many a soldier became an ex-soldier whose prospects outside the army were not overly promising; this was especially true for the ordinary privates, and their lack of education, transferable skills, and 'institutionalisation' meant later life became a challenge. A physically demanding life took its toll, and the wounds received rendered many infirm, and there were many of them. Discharge records of many Irish Waterloo veterans read like that of Private Patrick Molloy, County Wexford, 52nd Light Infantry, who was discharged in May 1823 at the age of 41, having been described as 'unfit' for military duties in consequence of age and length of service. He had been severely wounded in the right arm during the Waterloo campaign. There were many similar cases in the decades following Waterloo. Their pension, dependant on the length and nature of their service, did not necessarily prove adequate, and many were to suffer personal hardship.

Henry Magee of Donaghadee, County Down, died in April 1875, at the age of 94. A couple of years before this, some gentlemen of the locality appealed in *The Times* for subscriptions to a small fund for the old soldier, and twenty seven pounds, nine shillings and six pennies was thus raised to give some comfort to the veteran at the end of his days. A statement taken from him by D. Delacherois explained why he had no pension :

Henry Magee's statement in 1868. He enlisted at Lisburn, County Antrim under Lieutenant Clarke, Royal Artillery. A driver, 6th Battalion, Horse Artillery. Served under Colonel Wolfe at Waterloo; Captain Hayes was captain of the battery.

At Salamanca his arm was broken by a limber wheel – has now a stiff joint. Got bayonet wound in left leg; no scar can now be seen.

At Waterloo got musket ball wound in the right leg, scar still to be seen. Discharged in 1815 at Smithfield, London, having 8 years and 81 days service. Got no pension; was offered seven and a half pennies a day, but as other soldiers were getting two shillings and six pence a day for less wounds he says he made some angry remarks to the officer with the books, refusing so paltry a pension, and the result was he turned away with his discharge and got no pension. He has often since regretted his hasty and rude behaviour.

He was born in Killinchy, County Down, in November 1780, and is now 89 years of age. This statement is just as it was spoken by H Magee' – *The Irish Sword Vol VII, Summer 1965, No.26*

No, or insufficient, pension, no demand for his labour, and no work even if there was some often meant discharge was shortly followed by desperation, sometimes bringing ex – soldiers to the brink of illegality. Edward Costello, County Laois, 95th Rifles, discharged in 1819, found himself preparing to set an ambush to rob an unsuspecting by-passer, only chance decreed his first would-be victim was an old army comrade who instead helped him. Later matters turned even more fortuitously for him when another old comrade, a superior officer with whom he had served in Spain, and a fellow Waterloo veteran, George de Lacey Evans, saw that he eventually became a warden at the Tower of London.

Others were destined to have significant professional achievement, finding advancement and success both within the military and outside it. Lieutenant Colonel John Hammerton, County Tipperary, 44th Foot, who had been left for dead at Waterloo but for the attention of a loyal NCO, went on to be colonel-in-chief of the 55th Foot and afterwards was made a general. Major George O'Malley, County Mayo, 44th Foot, who took command of the regiment at Waterloo when Lieutenant Colonel Hammerton was wounded, went on to become commander of the Connaught Rangers. George de Lacey Evans, aide-de-camp to Major General Ponsonby at Waterloo, was also to achieve the rank of general, while Major Charles Rowan, County Antrim, 52nd Light Infantry, was afterwards Sir Charles Rowan KCB, Chief Commissioner of the Metropolitan Police. His younger brother, Sir William, a captain with the 52nd Light Infantry at Waterloo went on to become its colonel-in-chief. Many veterans, both commissioned and from the other ranks, veterans went on to live happy, active, lengthy lives long into the 19th century, having a range of differing experiences.

Never to know what the future had in store for them, however, were most of the 59th Regiment of Foot, who lost their lives on the night of 30 January 1816 when cruelly, after all the toils and dangers they had endured in the deliverance of Europe, their transport ship, *The Sea Horse*, broke into pieces after being driven by a storm into Tramore Bay; 298 men and 71 women and children perished in sight of land and witnessed by many. Only 30 men's lives were saved, the survivors seeing their comrades and relatives buried in one vast grave. That same night, in that same storm, off Ireland's south coast, another transport ship, *The Boadicea* was also lost, driven up onto rocks separating Garretstown and Garrylucas beaches just west of the Old Head of Kinsale, taking most of the 255 crew and 2nd Battalion of the 59th Regiment of Foot returning from the Waterloo campaign to garrison duty at Cork. A third ship, *The Lord*

Melville, carrying the 82nd Regiment of Foot, also struck rocks 300 yards off the Old Head but the vessel remained intact. Eventually those shipwrecked were saved by the men of Kinsale's Old Head Lighthouse. A rescue boat was launched but was overwhelmed by waves, all 12 occupants drowning in the deluge. On 30 January 1990, 184 years later to the day, after some stormy weather, a man walking along the beach near Garretstown noticed some human bones sticking out of the sand dunes. An inquiry soon suggested that these remains (of four bodies) may well have been belonging to those drowned more than a century and a half before.

The months after Waterloo were not all about ill-fated sea journeys, but one of the most famous was, of course, that taken by Napoleon into his final exile on St Helena on board the *HMS Bellerophon* in July 1815. On board as the ship's senior surgeon was Dr Barry Edward O'Meara from Blackrock, Dublin, educated at Trinity College Dublin and also at the Royal College of Surgeons. Formerly a medical member of the 62nd Regiment of Foot, he had some memorable experiences with them and later in the British Navy. Speaking excellent Italian and good French, the Irish doctor impressed Napoleon who requested that Dr O'Meara to become his personal physician. Dr O'Meara agreed to but on the strict understanding that he would look after Napoleon in his incarceration as his doctor and not as a spy. The sailing to St Helena took 72 days, ample time for both men to get to know each other and become friends. During the many monotonous days, weeks, months, and years the two men spent increasing amounts of time together discussing a wide variety of topics and subjects. Napoleon suggested to the doctor that he ought maintain a diary of events on the island, advising him, 'Doctor, it will make you a fortune, but please do not publish until after I am dead.' The arrival of a new governor general on the island, Sir Hudson Lowe, whom Napoleon took a dislike to, placed the Irishman in a position as 'go-between', which was to cause resentment with Lowe as the doctor was protective of his patient. Irritated by the Irishman's stance, Lowe sought to have him removed, in which case Napoleon would have refused to see any other doctor. The 'stand-off' lasted three years before Lowe's requests saw the eventual successful dismissal of the Irish doctor. In July 1818 the two friends bid farewell and Dr O'Meara arrived back to England, subsequently reporting to the Admiralty that Napoleon was ill and ought be brought to England for appropriate medical attention away from the isolated and wind-swept rock of an island permanently surrounded by cloud and mist. It was suggested to Dr O'Meara that he remain silent about Napoleon's health and he was offered a prestigious position which he said he would be pleased to take up 'when they remove my patient from St Helena'. He was cashiered from the Navy without pension and was struck off the medical register.

It was to be another Irish doctor, Dr James Roche Verling who had served as surgeon with the army during the Peninsular War, that Lowe sought to appoint. Only too aware of what had occurred previously, he felt he was placed in an untenable position. Highly conscious of the sensitive and apparently potentially dangerous position he faced, he was obviously reluctant to be in a situation where he could be accused of favouring the Emperor's party or acting in its interest. Verling did not want to become involved in having to report to Lowe any discussions heard expressed by the French, particularly in relation to matters concerning O'Meara. Caught between career and honour, between Lowe and the Emperor's party, Verling sought to quit St Helena and return to Britain. The eventual appointment of Dr Francesco Antommarchi, a Corsican, freed Verling from his plight. In the interim, the irrepressible Dr O'Meara rented up-market rooms in the centre of London, placed

Napoleon's wisdom tooth in the window, and practised successfully as a dentist. On Napoleon's death on St Helena on 5 May 1821, O'Meara edited down his diaries to two volumes, and they enjoyed a great circulation. Successful, famous,and wealthy, he lived until 12 July 1836.

AFTERWORD
– SO WHAT?

IT HAS been said that the two best developments for the British army during the 19th century were the introduction of Irish infantry and the invention of the breach-loading rifle. In Ireland, the British found and tapped a rich vein of manpower for their army, a convenient supply of ready troops. The Irish contributed greatly to Wellington's victories in the Peninsular War and at Waterloo, but it is a debt that has neither been recognised nor repaid.

'It is not too much to assert,' wrote Home Secretary Henry Addington, 1st Viscount Sidmouth, to the Lord Lieutenant of Ireland, Viscount Charles Whitworth, 'that the supply of troops from Ireland turned the scale on the 18th of June at Waterloo and without a fresh supply from the same quarter the Duke of Wellington cannot for a great length of time be again at a head of a British force.' *(24 June 1815)*

The trend continued so that by the mid-19th century Irish troops comprised over 40 percent of the British army, for the most part in the artillery and infantry. If, as it was, this continuing large-scale recruitment from Ireland did not change, neither was it that there was much innovation or improvement in the British army in the decades following Waterloo, Wellington and his generals simply seeing no need to change what had already served them well. There was no upgrading of medical services, equipment, organisation,or tactics in an army that went from 230,000 (1815) to 130,000 (1840). At Waterloo the British infantry had operated with a type of controlled frenzy, executing mechanically an intense concentration of fire. Napoleon's generals knew what Wellington could inflict on them so they had piled on the pressure, coming at the 'line of contact' in three separate waves, each massive in its own right, but they could not make them count. Wellington, clever and brave, and with his wit, clarity of thought, and self-confidence knew how to win, how to carry out 'running repairs' when matters seemed like they were going wrong. His reassuring sense of command and physical presence injected a sense of purpose, and despite the enormity of the occasion or crisis he seemed to infect those around him with a consummate belief in him and what he was about, and so in themselves. The fighting as it developed over the battle's nine-hour duration went through a number of clearly perceptible phases. These included three distinct and notably huge French attacks on Wellington's position: D'Erlon's massed infantry attack; Ney's massive cavalry charges; and the assault of the Imperial Guard. As these and other actions, critical moments and instances of great difficulty and danger, evolved and became extended, they dove-tailed, sometimes overlapped, or coincided with newly emerging struggles elsewhere on the battlefield. What became clear after the event was often confusing during it. In addition, fear and uncertainty are the enemies of clarity, they have an unsettling effect on logical reasoning, and can cause the most clear-headed to waver and prudent decision-making to suffer. Wellington fought the type of battle that he knew the British within the Anglo-Allied army was good at, and held his nerve. Together with the Prussians they defeated the French and history was shaped. Soon after sunrise on 19 June 1815 the full meaning of what had happened the day before started to become clear. Arguably, as a result of what happened at Waterloo, the 19th century was to be the century of the British as was the 20th century to be the century of the Americans, and today, for other reasons again, the 21st century is to be the century of China and Asia.

We Irish are more connected to the Battle of Waterloo than we are either aware of or understand. Perhaps a narrow narrative of our 'Irishness' and an over-simplistic view of our past heritage have distanced us from the historical fact that thousands of Irishmen fought, and fought bravely, at Waterloo. Reminders of Ireland's connections to Waterloo are still in plain sight, but symbolically invisible. This is perhaps understandable in light of the Irish nation's long struggle for freedom and self-determination, but now that this highly valued independence has been achieved, those monuments long ignored can once again be appreciated and interpreted in the way that was originally intended. Paradoxically, such monuments could be seen as an opportunity to demonstrate the nation's coming of age, proud and free Irish men and women acknowledging the Irish contribution to the freedom of Europe. The Battle of Waterloo was a conclusive end to over a quarter of a century of European instability; it ensured no single European power held exclusive sway; and the continent enjoyed substantive peace for the remainder of the 19th Century. Waterloo forged the modern identity of Europe. The Irish were at the Battle of Waterloo, they were there in sufficient numbers, and by their conduct in 'turning the scales on the 18th June', enhanced their Irish identity. Let Ireland and the Irish of the 21st century now do honour to these men by promoting a justified pride in them.

'It has been a damned serious business. Blücher
and I have lost thirty thousand men. It has been a
damned nice (close) thing – the nearest run thing
you ever saw in your life…By God! I don't think
it would have been done if I had not been there.'
 – The Duke of Wellington

THE 100 DAYS' CAMPAIGN, 1815
A CHRONOLOGY

01 MARCH

Napoleon escapes exile from Elba, lands in southern France.

20 MARCH   Napoleon enters Paris.

25 MARCH   Congress of Vienna declares war on Napoleon (not France). Prussia mobilises fastest, Austria and Russia take longer to organise larger armies.

15 JUNE   Napoleon's Armée du Nord makes surprise offensive into Belgium, crosses the Sambre river at Charleroi.

16 JUNE   0930 Wellington arrives at Quatre Bras. French preparing breakfast and waiting for orders.
1100 Napoleon arrives at Fleurus.
1200 Wellington meets Blücher at Brye.
1400 Battles of Ligny and Quatre Bras.

BATTLE OF LIGNY	BATTLE OF QUATRE BRAS
1500	French commence assault on villages	French advance halted by British.
1730	4 villages fell to French.	French cavalry charges, British infantry attack, British retake Bess Wood.
1900		Wellington counter-attacks, battle ends.
2030	French Imperial Guard breaks through Prussian centre. Blücher trapped under horse. Battle ends with victory for French.	No ground gained or lost by either side.

17 JUNE	'Fighting Retreat' to Mont-St-Jean. Outcome of Ligny, defeat of Prussians, made known to Wellington by ADC Gordon.
0930	Blücher determines Wavre as destination of retreat (Wellington's ADC Gordon present).
1030	Anglo-Allies retreat from Quatre Bras.
1100	Napoleon receives a report from Ney and orders him to attack Wellington. Grouchy is to pursue Blücher.
1200	Last of Anglo-Allies (rearguard) begins to leave Quatre Bras.
1300	Grouchy begins pursuit of the Prussians.
1430	Napoleon arrives at Quatre Bras to find British rearguard only and Ney's troops eating a meal. A summer thunderstorm begins.

1830	After encountering retreating British rearguard action, Napoleon's advance guard reaches La Belle Alliance.
2130	Wellington settles his army in the immediate environs of Mont-St-Jean and shelters from a severe overnight thunderstorm.

18 JUNE   **Battle of Waterloo**

0330	Wellington receives confirmation from Blücher that he will come to Mont-St-Jean. Wellington confirms he'll start at Mont-St-Jean.
0400	At dawn Prussians IV Corps begins to move towards Waterloo.
0900	Wellington deployment along Mont-St-Jean complete.
1000	Napolean orders his final dispositions.
1135	Battle begins. Cannonade commences (24-gun bombardment). Assault on Chateau Hougoumont.
1200	Grouchy decides not to 'March to the sound of guns'.
1300	Grand Battery opens up (80-plus gun bombardment). D'Erlon's massed French infantry assault on Anglo-Allied centre left. Attack is halted and countered with aid of British 2nd Heavy Cavalry Brigade. Charege a success, but continues 'to the (French) guns' repelled by French cavalry with 50% losses.
1600	Prussians IV Corps Advance Guard appears on French right emerging from the Bois de Paris. Ney's massive French cavalry attacks begin on Anglo-Allied line on the right

1730	Further French infantry attack on Allied centre at La Haye Sainte.
1830	Yet another French attack on La Haye Sainte; the farmhouse falls. A 'time of crisis' for Wellington. Ney asks for reinforcements – does not receive them. Some Imperial Guard units sent to Plancenoit.
1900	Arrival of Prussians (I Corps) near Wellington's left allowing him to contract his line, plug gaps and put in his last reserves.
1930	Assault of Imperial Guard on Anglo-Allied right centre. Attack is held in check and Anglo-Allies centre charge.
2030	Battle over.
2130	Prussians at Rossomme.
2200	The two victors, Wellington and Blücher, meet briefly at La Belle Alliance.
18/19 JUNE	Grouchy engages and wins 'Battle of Wavre', defeating Prussians III Corps, hears of French defeat at Waterloo and withdraws to France.
21 JUNE	Napoleon back in Paris, makes attempt to go to America.
15 JULY	Napoleon surrenders aboard *HMS Bellerophon* at La Rochelle.

APPENDICES

Strengths of the armies at Waterloo

French Armée du Nord:	Troops 78,000	Cannon 246 guns
Anglo-Allied Army:	Troops 73 000	Cannon 157 guns
Prussian Army:	Troops 50,000	Cannon 134 guns
TOTAL:	Troops 201,000	Cannon 537 guns

Losses at Waterloo (killed and wounded)

French Armée du Nord	30,000
Anglo-Allied Army	15,000
Prussian Army	7,000
TOTAL	52,000

British Regiments at Waterloo

1st Life Guards, now the Life Guards

2nd Life Guards, now the Life Guards

Royal Horse Guards, now the Blues and Royals

King's Dragoon Guards, now the Queen's Dragoon Guards

Royal Dragoons, now the Blues and Royals

APPENDICES

Royal Scots Greys, now the Royal Scots Dragoon Guards

6th Inniskilling Dragoons, later the 5th Inniskilling Dragoon Guards, and now the Royal Dragoon Guards

7th Hussars, later the Queen's Own Hussars and now the Queen's Royal Hussars

10th Hussars, later the Royal Hussars and now the King's Royal Hussars

11th Hussars, later the Royal Hussars and now the King's Royal Hussars

12th Light Dragoons, now the 9th/12th Lancers

13th Light Dragoons, later the 13th/18th King's Royal Hussars and now the Light Dragoons

15th Light Dragoons, later the 15th/19th Hussars and now the Light Dragoons

16th Light Dragoons, later the 16th/5th Lancers and now the Queen's Royal Lancers

18th Light Dragoons, later the 13th/18th King's Royal Hussars and now the Light Dragoons

Royal Artillery

Royal Engineers

1st Foot Guards, now the Grenadier Guards

2nd Coldstream Guards

3rd Foot Guards, now the Scots Guards

1st Foot, now the Royal Scots

4th King's Own Regiment of Foot, now the King's Own Royal Border Regiment

14th Foot, later the West Yorkshire Regiment and now the Prince of Wales's Own Regiment of Yorkshire

23rd Royal Welch Fusiliers

27th Foot, the Inniskilling Fusiliers and now the Royal Irish Regiment

28th Foot, later the Gloucestershire Regiment and now the Royal Gloucestershire, Berkshire and Wiltshire Regiment

30th Foot, later the East Lancashire Regiment and now the Queen's Lancashire Regiment

32nd Foot, later the Duke of Cornwall's Light Infantry and now the Light Infantry

33rd Foot, the Duke of Wellington's Regiment

40th Foot, later the South Lancashire Regiment and now the Queen's Lancashire Regiment

42nd Highlanders, now the Black Watch (the Royal Highland Regiment)

44th Foot, later the Essex Regiment and now the Royal Anglian Regiment

51st Light Infantry, later the King's Own Yorkshire Light Infantry and now the Light Infantry

52nd Light Infantry, later the Oxfordshire and Buckinghamshire Light Infantry and now the Royal Green Jackets

69th Foot, later the Welsh Regiment and now the Royal Regiment of Wales

71st Highland Light Infantry, now the Royal Highland Fusiliers

73rd Highlanders, the Black Watch

79th Highlanders, later the Queen's Own Cameron Highlanders, then the Queen's Own Highlanders and now the Highlanders

92nd Highlanders, the Gordon Highlanders and now the Highlanders

95th Rifles, later the Rifle Brigade and now the Royal Green Jackets

'The Waterloo Dispatch': Wellington's Report to the Secretary of State for War, Earl Bathurst

Waterloo, 19th June, 1815.

My Lord,

Buonaparte [sic], having collected the 1st, 2nd, 3rd, 4th and 6th corps of the French army, and the Imperial Guards, and nearly all the cavalry, on the Sambre, and between that river and the Meuse, between the 10th and 14th of the month advanced on the 15th and attacked the Prussian posts at Thuin and Lobbes, on the Sambre, at day-light in the morning.

I did not hear of these events till the morning of the 15th; and I immediately ordered the troops to prepare to march, and afterwards to march to their left, as soon as I had intelligence from other quarters to prove that the enemy's movement upon Charleroi was the real attack.

The enemy drove the Prussian posts from the Sambre on that day; and General Ziethen, who commanded the corps which had been at Charleroi, retired upon Fleurus; and Marshal Prince Blucher concentrated the Prussian army upon Sombref [sic], holding the villages in front of his position of St. Amand and Ligny.

The enemy continued his march along the road from Charleroi towards Bruxelles; and, on the same evening, the 15th, attacked a bridge of the army of the Netherlands, under the Prince de Weimar, posted at Frasne [sic], and forced it back to the farm house, on the same road, called Les Quatre Bras.

The Prince of Orange immediately reinforced this bridge with another of the same division, under General Perponcher, and, in the morning early, regained part of the ground which had been lost, so as to have the command of the communication leading Nivelles and Bruxelles with Marshal Blucher's position.

In the mean time, I had directed the whole army to march upon Les Quatre Bras; and the 5th division, under Lieut. General Sir Thomas Picton, arrived at about half past two in the day., followed by the corps of troops under the Duke of Brunswick, and afterwards by the contingent of Nassu.

At this time the enemy commenced an attack upon Prince Blucher with his whole force, excepting the 1st and 2nd corps, and a corps of cavalry under General Kellermann, with which he attacked our post at Les Quatre Bras.

The Prussian army maintained their position with their usual gallantry and perseverance against a great disparity of numbers, as the 4th corps of their army, under General Bulow, had not joined: and I was not able to assist them as I wished, as I was attacked myself, and the troops, the cavalry in particular, which had a long distance to march, had not arrived.

We maintained our position also, and completely defeated and repulsed all the enemy's attempts to get possession of it. The enemy repeatedly attacked us with large body of infantry and cavalry, supported by numerous and powerful artillery. He made several charges with the cavalry upon our infantry, but all were repulsed in the steadiest manner.

In this affair, His Royal Highness the Prince of Orange, the Duke of Brunswick, and Lieut. General Sir Thomas Picton, and Major Generals Sir James Kempt and Sir Denis Pack, who were engaged from the commencement of the enemy's attack, highly distinguished themselves, as well as Lieut. General Charles Baron Alten, Major General Sir C. Halkett, Lieut. General Cooke, and Major General Maitland and Byng, as they successively arrived. The troops of the 5th division, and those of the Brunswick corps, were long and severely engaged, and conducted themselves with the utmost gallantry. I must particularly mention the 28th, 42nd,

79th and 92nd regiments, and the battalion of Hanoverians.

Our loss was great, as your Lordship will perceive by the enclosed return; and I have particularly to regret His Serene Highness of Brunswick, who fell fighting gallantly at the head of his troops.

Although Marshal Blucher had maintained his position at Sombref [sic], he found himself much weakened by the severity of the contest in which he had been engaged, and, as the 4th corps had not arrived, he determined to fall back and to concentrate his army upon Wavre; and he marched in the night, after the action was over.

This movement of the Marshal rendered necessary a corresponding one upon my part; and I retired from the farm of Quatre Bras upon Genappe, and thence upon Waterloo, the next morning, the 17th, at ten o'clock.

The enemy made no effort to pursue Marshel Blucher. On the contrary, a patrole [sic] which I sent to Sombref in the morning found all quiet; and the enemy's vedettes fell back as the patrole advanced. Neither did he attempt to molest our march to the rear, although made in the middle of the day, excepting by following, with a large body of cavalry brought from his right, the cavalry under the Earl of Uxbridge.

This gave Lord Uxbridge an opportunity of charging them with the 1st Life Guards, upon their debouche (emergence) from the village of Genappe, upon which occasion his Lordship has declared himself to be well satisfied with that regiment.

The position which I took up in front of Waterloo crossed the high roads from Charleroi and Nivelles, and had its right thrown back to a ravine near Merke Braine [sic], which was occupied, and its left extended to a height above the hamlet of Ter la Haye, which was likewise occupied. In front of the right centre, and near the Nievelles road, we occupied the house and garden of Hougoumont, which covered the return of that flank; and in front of the left centre we occupied the farm of La Haye Sainte. By our left we communicated with Marshal Prince Blucher at Wavre, through Ohain; and the Marshal had promised me that, in case we should be attacked, he would support me with one or more corps, as might be necessary.

The enemy collected his army, with the exception of the 3rd corps, which had been sent to observe Marshal Blucher, on a range of heights in our front, in the course of the night of the 17th and yesterday morning, and at about ten o'clock he commenced a furious attack upon our post at Hougoumont. I had occupied that post with a detachment from General Byng's brigade of Guards, which was in position in its rear; and it was for some time under the command of Lieut. Colonel Macdonell, and afterwards of Colonel Home; and I am happy to add that it was maintained throughout the day with the utmost gallantry by these brave troops, notwithstanding the repeated efforts of large bodies of the enemy to obtain possession of it.

This attack upon the right of our centre was accompanied by a very heavy cannonade upon our whole line, which was destined to support the repeated attacks of cavalry and infantry, occasionally mixed, but sometimes separate, which wad made upon it. In one of these the enemy carried the farm house of La Haye Sainte, as the detachment of the light battalion of the German Legion, which occupied it, had expended all its ammunition; and the enemy occupied the only communication there was with them.

The enemy repeatedly charged our infantry with his cavalry; but these attacks were uniformly unsuccessful; and they afforded opportunities to our cavalry to charge, in one of which Lord E. Somerset's brigade, consisting of the Life Guards, the Royal Horse Guards, and (the) 1st dragoon guards, highly distinguished themselves, as did that of Major General Sir William Ponsonby, having taken many prisoners and an eagle.

These attacks were repeated till about seven in the evening, when the enemy made a desperate effort with cavalry and infantry, supported by the fire of artillery, to force our left centre, near the farm of La Haye Sainte, which, after a severe test, was defeated; and, having observed that the troops retired from this attack in great confusion, and that the march of General Bulow's corps, by Frischermont [sic], upon Planchenois [sic]and La Belle Alliance, had begun to take effect, and I could perceive the fire of his cannon, and as Marshal Prince Blucher had joined in person with a corps of his army to the left of our line by Ohain, I determined to attack the enemy, and immediately advanced the whole line og infantry, supported by the cavalry and artillery. The attack succeeded in every point: the enemy was forced from his positions on the heights, and fled in the utmost confusion, leaving behind him, as far as I could judge, 159 pieces of cannon, with their ammunition, which fell into our hands.

I continued the pursuit till long after dark, and then discounted it only on account of the fatigue of our troops, who had been engaged during twelve hours, and because I found myself on the same road with Marshal Blucher, who assured me of his intention to follow the enemy throughout the night. He has sent me word this morning that he has taken 60 pieces of cannon belonging to the Imperial Guard, and several carriages, baggage,&c., belonging to Buonaparte, in Genappe.

I propose to move this morning upon Nivelles, and not to discontinue my operations.

Your Lordship will observe that such a desperate action could not be fought, and such advantages could not be gained, without great loss; and I am sorry to add that ours has been immense. In

Lieut. General Sir. Thomas Picton His Majesty has sustained the loss of an officer who has frequently distinguished himself in his service; and he fell gloriously leading his division to a charge with bayonets, by which one of the most serious attacks made by the enemy on our position was repulsed. The Earl of Uxbridge after having successively got through this arduous day, received a wound by almost the last shot fired, which will, I am afraid, deprive His Majesty for some time of his service.

His Royal Highness the Prince of Orange distinguished himself by his gallantry and conduct, till ne received a wound from a musket ball through the shoulder, which obliged him to quit the field.

It gives me the greatest satisfaction to assure your Lordship that the army never, upon any occasion, conducted itself better. The division of Guards, under Lieut. General Cooke, who is severely wounded, Major General Maitland, and Major General Byng, set the example which was followed by all; and there is no officer nor description of troops that did not behave well.

I must, however, particularly mention, for His Royal Highness's (the Prince Regent's) approbation, Lieut. General Sir H. Clinton, Major General Adam, Lieut. General Charles Baron Alten (severely wounded), Major General Sir Colin Halkett (severely wounded), Colonel Ompteda, Colonel Mitchell (commanding a brigade of the 4th division), Major Generals Sir James Kempt and Sir D. Pack, Major General Lambert, Major General Lord E. Somerset, Major General Sir W. Ponsonby, Major General Sir C.Grant, and Major General Sir H. Vivian, Major General Sir J.O. Vandeleur, and Major General Count Dornberg.

I am also particularly indebted to General Lord Hill for his assistance and conduct upon this, as upon all former occasions.

The artillery and engineer departments were conducted much to my satisfaction by Colonel Sir George Wood and Colonel Smyth;

and I had every reason to be satisfied with the conduct of the Adjutant General, Major General Barnes, who was wounded, and od Quarter Master General Colonel De Lancey, who was killed by a cannon shot in the middle of the action [in fact he died of his wounds, eight days later]. This officer is a serious loss to His Majesty's service, and to me at this moment.

I was likewise much indebted to the assistance of Lieut. Colonel Lord Fitzroy [sic] Somerset, who was severely wounded, and of the officers composing his personal staff, who have suffered severely in this action. Lieut. Colonel the Hon. Sir Alexander Gordon, who has died of his wounds, was a most promising officer, and is a serious loss to His Majesty's service.

General Kruse, of the Nassu service, likewise conducted himself much to my satisfaction; as did BGeneral Tripp, commanding the heavy brigade of cavalry, and General Vanhope, commanding a brigade of infantry in the service of the King of the Netherlands.

General Pozzo di Borgo, General Baron Vicent, General Muffling, and General Alava, were in the field during the action, and rendered me every assistance in their power. Baron Vicent is wounded, but I hope not severely, and General Pozzo di Borgo received a contrusion.

I should not do justice to my own feelings, or to Marshal Blucher and the Prussian army, if I did not attribute the successful result of this arduous day to the cordial and timely assistance I received from them. The operation of General Bulow upon the enemy's flank was a most decisive one; and even if I had not found myself in a situation to make the attack which produced the final result, it would have forced the enemy to retire if his attacks should have failed, and would have prevented him from taking advantage of them if they should unfortunately have succeeded.

Since writing the above, I have received a report that Major

General Sir William Ponsonby is killed; and, in announcing this intelligence to your Lordship, I have to add the expression of my grief for the fate of an officer who had already rendered very brilliant and important services, and was an ornament to his profession.

I send with this dispatch three eagles(in fact, two), taken by the troops in this action, which Major Percy will have the honor of laying at the feet of His Royal Highness. I beg leave to recommend him to your Lordship's protection.

I have the honor to be, &c.

Wellington

Lists of Waterloo memorials of Irish interest

Waterloo Battlefield Memorial to the 27th Inniskillings ('The Skins').

Wellington Monument, Phoenix Park, Dublin.

Major General Denis Pack, 9th Brigade, St Canice's Church, Kilkenny.

Lieutenant Colonel (later Lieutenant General) John Hammerton, 44th Foot, Rathronan Cemetery near Clonmel, County Tipperary.

Major (later Major General) George O'Malley, 44th Foot, statue in Castlebar, County Mayo and memorial in Murrisk Cemetery near Castlebar.

Lieutenant Standish O'Grady, 7th Hussars, 2nd Viscount Guillamore (afterwards Colonel Viscount Guillamore, ADC to the Queen), St John's, Knockainey, Limerick.

Lieutenant John Vandeleur, 12th Light Dragoons, Stradbally North, Castleconnell, Limerick. He was the eldest son of John Ormsby Vandeleur of County Kildare by Frances Pakenham, sister of Edward Pakenham, 2nd Baron Longford, making John Vandeleur a first cousin of Kitty Pakenham the wife of Wellington.

Common terms and abbreviations

ADC: aide-de-camp.

CB: Knight Commander of the most Honourable Order of the Bath.

Ensign: Second Lieutenant.

Foot: Regiment of Foot.

GCH: Knight Grand Cross of Hanover.

KCH: Knight Commander of Hanover.

KH: Knight of Hanover.

KLG: The King's German Legion was a major British military unit raised by Lieutenant Colonel Johann Friedrich Vin der Decken and Major Colin Halkett on the order of King George III. The legion consisted mainly of officers and troops from the Electorate of Brunswick-Hanover which had been ruled by the monarch of Great Britain since 1714. The unit fought on several fronts during the Napoleonic Wars, including Waterloo, where under the high command of the Duke of Wellington and the direct command of Major Georg von Baring it defended the La Haye Sainte farmhouse. After the legion was disbanded in 1816, its soldiers to a large extent joined the armed forces of the newly established Kingdom of Hanover. Lieutenant William Shea from Cork was an officer with the German Legion.

N.C.O: Non-commissioned officer.

BIBLIOGRAPHY

Adkin, Mark, The Waterloo Companion: The Complete Guide to History's most Famous Land Battle (London, Aurum Press, 2001)

Brett-James, Antony, Life in Wellington's Army; (London, George Allen & Unwin Ltd, 1972

Chandler, David, Waterloo The Hundred Days, (Oxford, Osprey, 1980)

Childers, E.S.E. Major, The Story of The Rotal Hospital, Kilmainham (London)

Clayton, Tim, Waterloo (London, Little Brown, 2014)

Cornwell, Bernard, Waterloo The History of Four Days, Three Armies and Three Battles (London, William Collins Ltd, 2014)

Corrigan, Gordon, Waterloo A New History of the Battle and it's Armies. (London Atlantic Books, 2014)

Costello, Edward, The Adventures of a Soldier (London 1852)

Cotton, Edward, A Voice from Waterloo (London 1877)

Crane, David, Went the Day Well? Witnessing Waterloo (London, William Collins Ltd, 2015)

Dalton, Charles, The Waterloo Roll Call, (London, Arms and Armour Press, 1971)

Field, Andrew, Waterloo The French Perspective (Bransley, Pen & Sword Books Ltd, 2012)

Fox, Michael D, The Green Square: H.M. 27th (Inniskilling) Regiment of Foot at the Battle of Waterloo. (Kent, 1990)

Fremont-Barnes, Gregory, Waterloo 1815 The British Army's Day of Destiny, (Gloucestershire, The History Press, 2014)

Genet-Rouffiac, Nathalie, and Murphy, David (eds), Franco-Irish Military Connections, 1590-1945 (Dublin, 2009)

Haythornthwaite, Philip, British Napoleonic Infantry Tactics 1792-1815 (Oxford, Osprey, 2008)

Hofschroer, Peter, Wellington's Smallest Victory, The Duke, Th Model Maker and the Secret of Waterloo. (London, Faber and Faber, 2004)

Howorth, David, A Near Run Thing (London, Collins, 1968)

Keegan, John, The Face of Battle, A Study of Agincourt, Waterloo and the Somme. (London, The Bodley Head, 2014)

Lipscombe, Nick, Wellington's Guns, (Oxford, Osprey, 2013)

Longford, Elizabeth, Wellington, (London, Weidenfeld & Nicolson, 1992)

Mercer, Cavalie, Journal of the Waterloo Campaign, (2 Volumes, London, 1870)

Murphy, David, The Irish Brigade 1685-2006 (Dublin, 2007)

Pericoli, Ugo, 1815 The Armies at Waterloo, (London, Seeley, Service & Company, 1973)

Rogers, HCB Colonel, Wellington's Army, (London, Ian Allen Ltd, 1979)

Ross-Lewin, Harry, With "The Thirty-Second" in the Peninsular and other campaigns, edited by John Wardell (Dublin, 1804)

Siborne, H.T. The Waterloo Letters: Accounts of the Battle by British Officers for it'd foremost Historian (Oakpast, Leonaur, 2009)

Von Muffling, F.C.F, History of the Campaign of 1815, (Yorkshire, S.R. Publishers Ltd, 1970)

Weider, Ben and Hapgood, David, The Murder of Napoleon, (New York, Congdon & Lattes, INC, 1982)

Weller, Jac, Wellington at Waterloo, (London, Longmans, 1967)

Unpublished Thesis

Molloy, Peter, Ireland and the Waterloo Campaign of 1815, (M.A. Dissertation, National University of Ireland, Maynooth, 2011)

ACKNOWLEDGEMENTS

National Day of Commemoration, Royal Hospital Kilmainham, Dublin.

SHARP, STACCATO-SHOUTED orders of the officer-in-charge of the Irish Defence Forces Captain's Guard of Honour echoed loudly around the large cobblestoned courtyard and arcades of the Royal Hospital Kilmainham, its beautifully proportioned architecture underlining the dignity of the occasion: Ireland's National Day of Commemoration, which remembers all Irishmen and Irishwomen who died in past wars or on service with the United Nations. Falling annually on the Sunday nearest July 11, the anniversary of the date in 1921 that a truce ended the Irish War of Independence, it is marked by ceremonies throughout the country, the principal one being normally held at the Royal Hospital Kilmainham in Dublin. Escorted by a Captain's Guard of Honour, an Uachtarán (the Irish President) arrives at the ceremony and is received by the Irish Defence Forces Chief of Staff and General Officer Commanding 2nd Eastern Brigade and is conducted by them to a position facing the Regimental colour of the Captain's Guard of Honour. On completion, the Guard of Honour leaves the parade ground and the President invites the clergy to commence the prayer service. After the inter-denominational prayer service, the Parade Commander brings the parade to attention and then gives orders to the Cadet Honour Guard on Parade. When they have assumed their position the order is given to them to 'reverse arms'. The President lays a wreath which is followed by one minute of silence and the playing of the 'Last Post' by the Military Band. At this stage the national flag is raised to full mast and the Military Band plays 'Reveille' and the Cadet Guard of Honour presents arms. The ceremony is then closed by the playing of the National Anthem and as the last strains of it are played the Irish Air Corps completes a fly-over. The military and religious ceremony is held in the presence of the President, the Taoiseach, and other members of the Government, members of the Oireachtas, the Council of State, the Diplomatic Corps, the Judiciary, relatives of 1916 leaders, next-of-kin of those who died on service with the United Nations, Northern Ireland representatives, and a wide cross-section of the community, including ex-servicemen and servicewomen.

The Royal Hospital, built in an effort to go some way towards alleviating problems experienced in the later lives of Irish ex-soldiers who had served in the British army, was established by a Charter of Charles II in 1680 AD which stated that 'that such of the...army, as hath faithfully served...in the strength and vigour of their youth, may in the weakness, and disasters, that their old age, wounds or other misfortunes may bring them into, find a comfortable, retreat and a competent maintenance therein.'

Of the hundreds of thousands of Irishmen who left these shores to fight other people's battles, wearing other people's uniforms under other people's flags, some 367 are buried in the two burial grounds within the walls of the Royal Hospital, including those who fought at Waterloo – 'the bravest of the brave'. Sergeant James Graham, County Monoghan among them. Centuries later their martial spirits must surely feel a sense of pride as they are paid due recognition by their fellow countrymen and women in Ireland's national uniform under Ireland's national flag.

My life-long interest in the Battle of Waterloo began early and led to my first remembered 'Battle of Waterloo of my own' with my father, who despite my passionate persistence, refused on the grounds of my age to allow me to go to see Dino De Laurentiis's 1970 film *Waterloo* directed by Sergi Bondarchuk. I had to pass the Capitol Cinema (now gone) on Cork's Grand Parade twice daily going to and from school and content myself at marvelling at the magnificent poster, knowing I was not to see the film. I have seen it many times since, read most of the very, very many books on the subject, and have visited the battlefield on several occasions. It is true then when I tell you I feel humbled and honoured to write this account; it is by no means the definitive work, but nonetheless it is one of the first of its kind, and it is for me now to wholeheartedly acknowledge and thank all those who with their encouragement, input, advice and assistance gave willingly of their time, expertise and effort. Peter Molloy's thesis 'Ireland and the Waterloo campaign of 1815' for the National University of Ireland (Maynooth) in October 2011 was a very worthy starting point, the advice and direction of his supervisor, Dr David Murphy, further enhancing my endeavour and introducing me to Nicholas Dunne-Lynch whose ardour for the subject is infectious and matched by only the accuracy of his research. My sincere thanks to Barry Bradfield whose never-failing assistance and uncanny ability to unearth a wealth of valuable detail over many months has populated the pages of this important story, a tale that simply could not have been told without his expertise, interest, and unstinting enthusiasm, qualities for which I will be forever grateful; to Colonel Nick Lipscombe, Royal Artillery (retd) whose knowledge of Wellington's artillery was of great assistance; to Paul Evans Royal Artillery Museum Woolwich; to the staff of the Irish Defence Forces Library at the Military College, Curragh Camp; for assistance with imagery I wish to gratefully acknowledge the help of Anne Hodge, Maire Mc Feely, and Louise Morgan, the National Gallery of Ireland, Lar Joye, National Museum of Ireland, Lieutenant Colonel Tom Heskin (retd), and Corporal Wayne Fitzgerald of *An Cosantóir*, the Irish Defence Forces' Magazine; to Paul O'Brien, Office of Public Works at the Royal Hospital Kilmainham for sharing his knowledge on this valued building with it's fascinating history, Kenneth Ferguson, the Military History Society of Ireland, Richard Kilroy and Mike Bolton of the Old Wellingtonian Society in Ireland, Angela Dunne for her knowledge on the Wexford Harveys, Colonel Tuncay Semin, Turkish Military Academy, for his kind assistance in relation to the maps included to orient the reader and help illustrate the course of events; to Fintan O'Connell, Inspire Printers, Skibbereen, County Cork, and his excellent staff for their many preparations in putting this story on paper and the production of the book proper; to Jack and Barbara O'Connell, Schull Books, Ballydehob, County Cork, for their encouraging words and advice in the initial stages of this undertaking.; to Lynn, my second daughter for her artwork, produced to a high standard under pressure while concurrently coping with demands for her final year design degree, a special thank you; to Eva, Mary–Claire, and Hugo, my other children, for their encouragement, interest, and understanding, not to mention their patience and indulgence in having their father physically present but sometimes (often) mentally in Waterloo.

INDEX

A

Addington, Henry 113, 143

Alexander I, Tsar 16, 19

Anderson, Lieutenant Henry
  97

Armée du Nord *xii*, 30, 49, 52,
  147, 151

B

Baker Rifle 76

Barnard, Lieutenant Colonel Sir
  Andrew 58, 75, 90

Barnes, Major General 58, 160

Bauduin, General Pierre-
  François 69

Belcher, Lieutenant Robert
  Tresilion 80, 90

Bernard, Coronet Henry Boyle
  117

Black Watch 80

Blücher, Field Marshal Gebhard
  von iii, 30-33, 37, 38, 43, 45,
  46, 55-56, 58, 98, 106, 110,
  112, 116, 120, 146-150

Boyse, Captain Jaques 39

Boyse, Major Shetland 111

Braine l'Alleud 44, 105

Brown Bess musket 26, 76

Browne, Lieutenant John 123

Browne, Lieutenant the Honourable William 109

Brunswickers 108

Busteed, Lieutenant Christopher 97

C

Cahirmee horse fair 120, 121

Carroll, Private David 80

Cassen, Captain Thomas 39

Castlereagh, Viscount 8, 16

Cheeseman, Lieutenant 9

Clarke, Ensign William
  Aldworth 125

Coldstream Guards *xi*, 65, 68,
  71, 73, 90, 131, 136, 152

Cole, General Sir Galbraith
  Lowry 58

Colthurst, Lieutenant James 51

Connaught Rangers 9, 139

Cooke, Ensign Peter 81

Cornwallis, Lord 7

Costello, Private Edward *x*, 38-
  40, 51, 75, 123, 135, 138

Cotter, Captain George 35, 51,
  52, 97

Creevey, Thomas 3

Cross, Captain John 109

D

Dawson, Lieutenant Colonel
  John 34, 90, 111

D'Erlon, General Jean-Baptiste